Little Smoky
Ridge

Little Smoky Ridge

THE NATURAL HISTORY OF A SOUTHERN APPALACHIAN NEIGHBORHOOD

Marion Pearsall

1959

UNIVERSITY OF ALABAMA PRESS

Preface

THE NAME "LITTLE SMOKY RIDGE" AND THE NAMES OF
all persons and most places mentioned in the following
pages are fictitious. The neighborhood, however, is real.
Or it was real several years ago when the study began.
Since that time many of the changes foreshadowed then
have come to pass. There has been a slight overall decrease in population, but more significant is the reorien-
tation of relationships between households through
deaths, marriages, and the movement of whole families
in or out of the separate geographic segments that, in
1949, were loosely organized into a neighborhood unit.

By 1956, one of the smaller hollows was deserted and
households along the other branches had either become
more isolated or, in a few cases, had extended their ties
with families and neighborhoods that formerly were entirely separate. There has been no further extension of
outside agencies into the neighborhood itself. In fact,
Little Smoky Ridge is, if anything, more isolated from
outside influence now than it was several years ago. The

behavior of new families suggests that perhaps this kind of remote neighborhood furnishes a sort of last refuge for those who will not or cannot meet the prevailing standards of modern American life.

Use of the present tense here, unless otherwise speci-fied, applies to the initial period of fieldwork during the summer, fall, and early winter of 1949-50. For about two months of the summer I lived in the neighborhood, making daily visits to the various households and par-ticipating as fully as possible in all activities. After ex-plaining my interest in learning about the old ways, the histories of the different families, and especially in find-ing out how life had changed since the time of the first settlers, I was able to conduct more or less formal inter-views with most of the families. I also took part in local religious services sponsored by a mission center and as-sisted in a number of immunization clinics in Little Smoky Ridge and other parts of the county. In the fall I moved to a house several miles from the neighborhood but continued daily visits to the Ridge, "staying the day" at first one house and then another and attending all gatherings that brought the several families together.

The original decision to study a Southern Appalachian neighborhood was more accidental and personal than strictly scientific. Justification for the choice lies in a conviction that the American hinterland may be as in-structive to the student of social and cultural change as any primitive or peasant society elsewhere. And there is the added pleasure of discovering a special part of one's own culture, one of the many subcultures that together make the complexity of American society.

The selection of Little Smoky Ridge rather than a more "representative" Appalachian settlement was both fortunate and unfortunate. It was fortunate in that the neighborhood is small enough for a single observer to comprehend its essential features, and it is isolated enough to represent very largely a single cultural tradition. On the other hand, it does not reflect the present conditions as found in most parts of the region.

Little Smoky Ridge is representative of only a small segment of the Southern Appalachian population of today. More than most neighborhoods, it has suffered the abrasions of extreme poverty through several generations in a physical and social environment that prohibits any foreseeable improvement of conditions. Yet there are at least half a dozen similar neighborhoods in the same county and as many in adjacent counties, not to mention the probability that all the more mountainous counties of the region have a few such sections. Good roads, developing industries, and closer communication with other parts of the country have reduced the number of Little Smoky Ridges; but their continued existence at all has implications for understanding the process of acculturation where an already precariously balanced native society meets a highly organized commercial-industrial civilization.

The effects of this meeting of cultures provide the rather tragic central theme of the present study. As stated in Chapter Four, "Little Smoky Ridge stands as a twentieth century illustration of the persistence of a frontier type of social organization and value system in an environment no longer suited to either." Trends inherent in the original culture began to undermine its balance to the natural environment almost from the beginning, and continued isolation prevented the introduction of technological and social measures that might have arrested the course of events before irreparable damage was done. Instead, the trends continued until today an almost unbridgeable gap exists between local ways and means and the ways and means of a larger American culture which has finally reached Little Smoky Ridge. The neighborhood itself seems doomed, and there is some doubt as to the success its individual families may have in modifying their traditional behavior.

In presenting the story of Little Smoky Ridge in the following chapters, I have tried to place the events of its appearance, growth, and present decline against a larger background of space and time and regional cultural change. The method is essentially that of natural history which seeks to understand facts as they occur through time in a natural setting. There is first an attempt to record the facts objectively and classify them logically. More important, there is a search for meaningful relationships and an understanding of processes which, once defined, will be applicable to all phenomena of the same general class. In organizing the data to see the relations and trends that give them meaning I have used some common anthropological assumptions about the kind of necessary adjustments which all societies must make if they are to survive and which they can only make by cultural means.

Thus, Chapters Two, Three, and Four deal primarily with the fundamental adjustment of the society to its physical environment. Chapter Six, then, considers in more detail the traditional social organization and the means whereby members of the society relate to each other to accomplish the goals of their culture. There are special value systems supporting both the relation to the environment and the relation to other members of the society, but there are also values that give meaning to everything else through imparting a sense of ultimate dependence on forces outside the realm of nature or man. These supernatural sanctions are discussed especially in Chapter Seven. Since the ways of adjusting to nature, to man, and to the supernatural are interrelated, there is necessarily considerable overlapping of content between chapters.

The ultimate fate of the neighborhood, of course, depends upon its relations with and adjustments to other social and cultural systems. Chapters Five, Nine, and Ten consider the relationships which exist between Little

Smoky Ridge and the outside world. My data on this aspect of neighborhood life are unfortunately incomplete since the original study was conceived along narrower lines than the present report. I have had to draw on studies by other investigators, especially for information on the adjustment of migrants from the Southern Appalachians to industrial centers. My own more limited evidence, however, is entirely consistent with their findings.

Finally, I am aware of the unique reality of Little Smoky Ridge and its people and have tried throughout to let a human dimension throw additional light on the cultural interpretation. For while the goal of scientific analysis is generalization, much of the flavor of life in a given human group lies in the myriad detail of behavior as personality responds to personality from day to day. It was the unique and personal detail that gave zest and color to the fieldwork in Little Smoky Ridge and created the friendships I cherish. It was impossible to write about the neighborhood without mentioning the people.

M. P.

Acknowledgments

FOR FINANCIAL ASSISTANCE DURING A YEAR OF FIELD-
work and the writing of a first report in the form of a
doctoral dissertation I wish to thank the Department of
Anthropology of the University of California at Berke-
ley. Grateful acknowledgment of aid through another
season of fieldwork and background research is due the
Wenner-Gren Foundation for Anthropological Research
of New York.

I also wish to express a debt of personal gratitude to
Professors Robert H. Lowie, David G. Mandelbaum, and
Robert A. Nisbet, whose guidance and encouragement
in the first period of work made possible the present report. Finally, I am indebted to many friends, col-
leagues, and students who have listened patiently to my
enthusiastic reports of the Southern Appalachian region
in general and of Little Smoky Ridge in particular.
They have helped to shape the ideas presented here, al-

though I must accept the final responsibility for fact
and interpretation myself.

Marion Pearsall,
University of Kentucky

Contents

CHAPTER ONE

Introducing the Neighborhood

AS A SOCIAL AND CULTURAL ENTITY LITTLE SMOKY Ridge closely resembles many other impoverished neighborhoods in the Southern Appalachians. It has some special features, but even these are paralleled in other parts of the region. For example, a Protestant mission has considered the Ridge part of its charge for more than thirty years and has maintained a small chapel in the neighborhood for more than twenty years. The mission, which began as an evangelical and educational center at nearby Russell Cove, has influenced the area, though not always in the way it intended. Like many other missions of various denominations in the Southern mountains it has provided religious, educational, and medical services by missionary workers recruited mainly from other parts of the country and exhibiting varying degrees of sympathy for local custom.

The neighborhood is also special in its relation to the Great Smoky Mountains National Park, for some of the present residents formerly lived on land now incorporated in the park. They speak bitterly of the Govern-

ment that took away all the "best" land. Again, there
are many other parts of the region that have also witnessed displacement of population in the development
of parks, forests and reservoirs.

Another feature of Little Smoky Ridge throws light
on the special relations between different types of neighborhoods within the region. Little Smoky "on the mountain" is considered backward and primitive by people
living "on the creek" and "down river." People along
the creek point to residents of the Ridge as lazy and
shiftless. The storekeeper mutters that there is no use in
the mission trying to help people like that. They will
never change. Individuals "back on the mountain" are
"characters." They are the butt of jokes and gibes,
mostly not malicious, for there is an element of pity
even when disgust is expressed for their habits. There
is a pleasant sense of superiority, and the creek dweller
can afford to close an account of mountain peculiarities
with the charitable phrase, "I guess I'd be as queer as
her if I'd lived back there all my life."

Although Little Smoky Ridge has much in common
with some other mountain neighborhoods and has problems which are shared by a certain segment of the region's population, it is unique in the sense that its
conditions are not exactly duplicated elsewhere. And
within the neighborhood itself, conditions are not exactly the same from one period to another. As friendships change or as marriages and moving alter social

relations, the boundaries of the neighborhood also shift.

Little Smoky Ridge is today a neighborhood only in the very loose sense of a group of houses in which there are social relations between families and individuals. More specifically, it is a group of about twenty houses with a fluctuating population of from 100 to 120 persons. Most of the families attend the same churches. That is, they all go to two or three churches in the vicinity, depending on where and when meetings are held and who is preaching. The churches are identified with particular neighborhoods but draw listeners from several. Most of the children attend the same school, but the school also serves more than one neighborhood. Similarly, the three or four country stores and as many grist and saw mills patronized by people from Little Smoky Ridge serve wider areas.

In social relations, persons living on the Ridge have more contacts with each other than with any outside group. However, blood and friendship ties and geographic propinquity unite some families rather closely with hollows to the west, while the interests of other families extend to the east. Many share some interests and activities with people along the creeks and, in a more limited way, with families scattered throughout the mountainous portions of East Tennessee and western North Carolina. Contacts with larger population centers are of a more impersonal nature. Individuals market crops, shop and sometimes work in Holston and Thomasville, the two nearest county seat towns, and in White City, the nearest large trade center.

A small isolated neighborhood of closely related members all engaged in similar occupations does not present the range of individual variability that might be expected in a larger society with a more elaborate division of labor. Nevertheless, the society is one in which individualism and independence of person are valued and in which strong personalities are the rule. It may not be amiss to introduce a few of the neighbors as they would be met on a trip up Rocky Branch to the top of the Ridge and down Roaring Branch on the other side, then back through a narrow break near the base of the mountain to Morgan Branch. (See the accompanying diagrammatic map and key to households, page 6.)

Sula McCoy lives at the foot of Rocky Branch, nearly a mile back from the creek road. Illiterate and untraveled, Sula is completely unaware that she is the object of pity from anyone. A former mission minister used her as a contemporary illustration of the "widow's mite." He described her, barefoot and ragged, one baby on her hip and another toddling beside, as she came forward to give a nickel for relief of the poor and needy in India. The story may be apocryphal; it is certainly in character.

Sula's relations with men have been stormy. She was a Brown before marriage, and her first child is a Brown for want of a better name. She later married and quickly divorced a Weber. For the past dozen years she has had an off and on marriage with Print McCoy. In Sula's version of the marriage, Print is a "terrible man." He drinks, beats her, and frequently "takes a gun" to her. From one of these episodes she barely escaped with her life and fled over the mountain. But a reconciliation was effected even after that incident.

It is impossible to verify all the details of Sula's story. They are recorded as given by her because they illustrate a common characteristic of the neighborhood. Incidents take on details of violence in the retelling. The teller pictures himself as virtuous and justified. He is always, for some unaccountable reason, terribly put upon and offended against by the other party. There is no middle ground or suggestion of personal guilt.

As for Print, he seems mild and polite enough. He recites tales of suffering at the hands of neighbors to anyone who will listen. His neighbors are always shooting at him or his children. They killed two mules that belonged to him. They deliberately let their cow loose in his corn. His fantasies are only remotely grounded in fact. One of the mules, for example, simply died of overwork and old age. Although Print is suspicious of his immediate neighbors, he enjoys entertaining friends with his homemade whiskey. He is not a bootlegger, but some of his corn is always destined for liquid consumption.

For several years the John Bruton family lived above

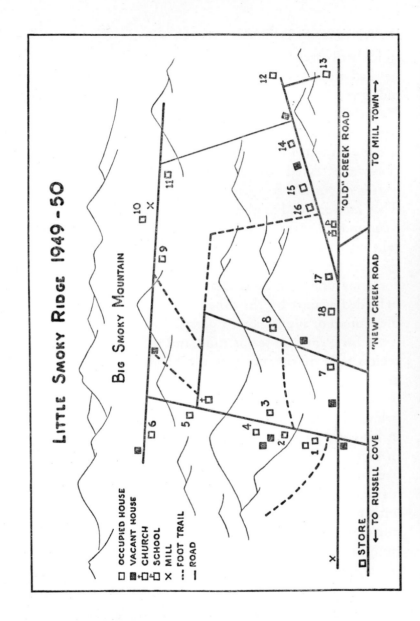

LITTLE SMOKY RIDGE 1949-50

BIG SMOKY MOUNTAIN

OCCUPIED HOUSE
VACANT HOUSE
CHURCH
SCHOOL
MILL
FOOT TRAIL
ROAD

STORE

← TO RUSSELL COVE

"NEW" CREEK ROAD

"OLD" CREEK ROAD

TO MILL TOWN →

KEY TO HOUSEHOLDS, LITTLE SMOKY RIDGE (1949-50)

1. Print and Sula McCoy. 4 children.
2. John and Martha Bruton. 7 Children.
3. Lige and Cora Floyd. 1 grown son, 7 children.
4. Eliza Bruton. 2 grown sons.
5. Eph and Lily Morgan. Eli Morgan.
6. Lon Brown.
7. Clyde and Sarah Stinnot. 2 children.
8. Jay and Pearl Weber. 2 children.
9. Jim and Maggie Jones. 1 grown son, his wife and 5 children.
10. Robert and Elva Johnson. 5 children.
11. Orville and Lena Jones. 1 grown son, 4 children.
12. Dan Johnson. 1 grown daughter, her 2 children.
13. Mat and Ruth Morgan. 1 grown daughter with 2 children, 4 children.
14. Jim and Molly Morgan. 1 grown daughter, 4 children.
15. Elmer and Dora Morgan. 2 grown sons, 1 grown daughter.
16. Will and Jennie McCoy. 3 grown sons, 1 child.
17. Wes and Mina Randolph. 1 grown daughter with 1 child, 2 children.
18. John and Jean Mason. 5 children.

Note: Persons under age 16 are listed as children.

the McCoys and added fuel enough to keep Print's fantasies burning. They moved away from the neighborhood in 1950, but they may be expected to return at
any time since John knows he may always return to his
mother's land.

John's family illustrates the fact that even such a
neighborhood, small and seemingly on one social level,
has its social distinctions. The family was generally
considered dirty, beggarly and untruthful. They were
not welcome in other homes, and no one visited in
theirs. Of the seven children, four had noticeable physical defects. Of the youngest, John's mother says in
a tone of accepting the inevitable, "They'll never raise
that young one."

Across the hollow from the John Bruton house lives
Lige Floyd, a shrewd patriarch of an older generation
who rules his large family with an iron hand. He is a
good provider and demands in return the respect and
obedience of those for whom he provides. He has refused at times to let his children attend school or Sunday
school in the firm belief that these institutions do more
harm than good. He saw the value of education only
after hints that his welfare check might be withheld if
the children did not appear regularly in school. Nothing
has convinced him of the value of formal religion and
he remains the only real doubter in a strongly Protestant
Christian neighborhood. He argues that there are too
many different pictures of Christ to be believable be-

cause "you know if there was such a person, they'd know what he looked like."

Eliza Bruton, known generally as "Aunt" Eliza, lives on land adjoining her half-brother Lige on one side and her son John on the other side. All three places are on land originally belonging to a mutual ancestor, Jim Floyd. In spite of their kinship, Lige and Eliza are not always on friendly terms. For years they kept alive a dispute over a spring between the two houses. Lige claimed the spring was on his land and refused Eliza the use of it. She in turn took every opportunity to spit in the spring whenever she thought he was watching.

Eliza's ways and speech are those of two or three generations ago which means they are essentially the ways of the early American frontier. She has been choosy about adopting modern American culture as it has come within her view. She has a battery radio, for instance, and enjoys the "pretty racket" of hillbilly programs. "Those crazy women" in the soap operas, however, receive short shrift from Eliza. They are too silly and their men folk ought to whip them.

Eliza has lived her life in an area extending less than twenty miles in any direction from her present home and she now intends to move no farther than to a grave beside her husband at the top of the mountain. Two sons have tried to take her to live with them, but she reckons she will die alone where she is. There are days when she feels sorry for herself and talks of the eleven

children she has borne and raised, nine of them still living. Now they have deserted her in unfilial ingratitude.
Two sons are unmarried and should by rights look after
her. Typically, she states the case one-sidedly. When
the boys are home Eliza enjoys violent arguments as
much as they and contributes enthusiastically to discord.
But she is quick to defend her children against accusations from outsiders.

An incident which occurred several years ago illustrates Eliza's attitude toward her sons. She "lawed"
San, the older of the boys at home. The "law" in this
instance was a local constable and neighbor. The situation cannot be compared to an urban mother calling on
an impersonal police force. San had been drinking and
came home to tear up the house. He broke a lamp
against the wall and carried the kitchen range out of the
house to smash it in the yard. So Eliza got the "law" to
order him to return the stove and to clean it first, the
only time it has been thoroughly cleaned. Now the
stove is dirty again and Eliza jokes to San, "You better
get you a jar of whiskey; the stove needs cleaning."

Both San and Lum, the other bachelor son, are home
as much as they are away. They come and go as they
please, as do most men of the neighborhood. Restlessness
sends them squirrel hunting or drinking or looking for
work. Sometimes the explanation is, "They've near
lawed poor Lum to death, and he had to go to North

Carolina." When they have had enough of wandering, they appear at home again.

The house at the top of Rocky Branch is occupied by Eph and Lily Morgan. Lily is sister to Sula McCoy at the foot of the Branch, and Eph's family gave its name to Morgan Branch. Lily and Eph are childless after eight or ten years of marriage, and their childless condition may account in part for the fact that they seem closer than most couples. Lily has time to keep her house spotless and still join Eph as he works on the mountain or goes to the store. When men gather in the yard or on the porch, Lily is more often included in their conversation than are most women.

For some time before his death in 1949, "Uncle" Eli Morgan, Eph's grandfather, lived with Eph and Lily. Of all his children and grandchildren, they had the most room for him; and his old age assistance checks were a welcome addition to their tiny and uncertain income. "Uncle" Eli was an old-timer whose childhood was spent in the dark days following the Civil War. In early manhood he, like many of his generation, worked intermittently on "public works," as the large lumbering operations were termed. He never cared too much for the work, but "it gave a man a chance to support his family." The only job he really liked was guarding the machinery from bears that had a taste for engine grease. Eli freely admitted to being a terrible sinner in his youth, fiddling and attending "frolics." Later he was converted and became a preacher and exhorter, traveling miles to conduct prayer meetings in many of the neighborhoods and small settlements of the area.

From the top of Rocky Branch, one descends to the head of Roaring Branch to Lon Brown's house. Brother of Sula McCoy and Lily Morgan, Lon was always the "puny" member of the family. As a boy, Lon spent many months in a Johnson City hospital being treated for osteomyelitis. His mother had doctored a cut on his leg with powdered charcoal, the accepted local remedy. After severe infection started, a medical doctor was called, and the doctor made arrangements for Lon's hospitalization. Lon learned to read a little in the hospital, a skill he now reserves mainly for deciphering title labels on his phonograph records.

Lon's house is a gathering place for young people of both sexes. This may be partly because he lives alone and there are no older people to restrict activities. But age distinctions are not important in the neighborhood, and the main attraction is his collection of records of popular ballads and religious songs as recorded by well known hillbilly artists.

Lon works occasionally on farms along the creek but does almost nothing on his own land. When three or four straggly stalks of corn persisted in growing in his yard, he joked that he was going to have to get someone to pull fodder for him "on halves."

Farther down Roaring Branch Jim and Maggie Jones have a farm which is a few acres larger and considerably flatter than most. Jim also runs a small sawmill so they are easily the most prosperous couple in the neighborhood. They serve a greater variety and greater abundance of food than their neighbors. They have a small organ in their living room. And Maggie has a matching set of six plates. Aside from such details, there is little to set them apart.

Maggie exemplifies many local values. Strong-minded and strong-bodied, it is her boast that she has done every kind of work except plowing and splitting rails. For these tasks she is too short. She has a deep love for the mountains, for every flower, bird and butterfly on her land. She knows town life would be unbearable. She is also deeply religious; her God goes with her through every day as she hums hymns to herself. The "renewal" of Jim at a prayer meeting in 1951 has given her new peace for she had worried about the fate of his soul if he should die suddenly.

Jim and Maggie are now alone most of the time. Their four children are grown and married, but two of the sons live farther down the branch. For several months in 1949 and 1950, one son and his entire family lived at home while waiting for the farm below to be vacated. There was nothing unusual in the moving arrangements, although they affected three or four families. B. J. Jones wanted to return to the neighborhood

after an absence. He could move into the house then
occupied by Robert Johnson. The Robert Johnsons
were going to move to a house occupied by the Jim
Morgans, who were planning to move into a vacant house
below Elmer Morgan. Eventually the shifts were completed to the satisfaction of all.

From Roaring Branch a short trail leads past Dan
Johnson's to Morgan Branch. Dan is one of the oldest
inhabitants, half-brother to "Uncle" Eli Morgan at the
top of Rocky Branch. He is a woodcarver of considerable skill, and his work has been exhibited at fairs for
Southern Appalachian handicrafts. Dan is a "most contented" man, too contented of late to bother to fill orders for his carvings. A daughter whose husband left
her keeps house for Dan, and her two adolescent sons
complete the household.

The Mat Morgans live in a tiny mountain cove
nestled between the rugged base ridges of Big Smoky
Mountain. The site is beautiful, and the Morgans fully
appreciate its beauty. Mrs. Morgan wishes for a larger
house, but otherwise seems more than satisfied. The
house is log and old, with only one room for the nine
members of the family, but it is always neat.

The Morgans are a co-operative family unit of the
sort that a generation ago could have been almost entirely self-sufficient. Under present conditions they
struggle to maintain a bare subsistence, always in need

of a little outside help . Mat used to work in White City, walking and hitchhiking the 45 miles home every week-end. Late in 1950 he suffered an injury and has stayed home since.

Two daughters still living at home illustrate different aspects of a problem that many of the younger genera-tion face. Both have lived in town for a while, but with different reactions. Mary, the elder, lived in White City with her husband and hated town life. She finally persuaded her husband to return to the mountains, where he soon rejoined old moonshining companions, and she left him.

The other daughter, an attractive young adolescent, enjoyed her stay with relatives in White City. The city had many attractions for a vivacious girl craving a little excitement. Home ties were strong, too, and the girl finally returned. Perhaps it is no coincidence that, soon after her return, she fell into a weeping fit at a prayer meeting. She was convinced she had strayed from God and fallen into sin. Long and loud prayers finally re-stored her peace of mind, and she "came through for Jesus."

In the next Morgan household Elmer, two grown sons, and a third unrelated young man are engaged in moon-shining much of the time, as are about a dozen other men in the neighborhood. The younger men are in-clined to be trouble-makers when they have been sampling their wares, but Elmer exerts his authority to keep them in line. It is Elmer's wife, however, who really rules the family with her tongue.

Elmer has a sister, Jennie McCoy, who lives a quarter of a mile farther down the branch. She is a tall, handsome woman with an air of quiet dignity. She would be surprised that she is "poor Jennie," just as her sister-in-law on the first branch is "poor Sula," to better-situated families along the creek. Jennie knows her life is hard and her family could use more food and clothing than they have, but she has a calm acceptance of circumstances.

I have mentioned approximately half the households. They represent the range of neighborhood existence from the smallest to the largest family, from poorest to most prosperous, from most conservative to most progressive in customary behavior and values. Later chapters will describe the way of life on Little Smoky Ridge in detail, but the contemporary scene will not be completely understandable without a consideration of the geographic setting and historical background.

CHAPTER TWO

The Setting

LITTLE SMOKY RIDGE FAMILIES LIVE ALONG THE DEEP
V-shaped valleys that cut and drain the steep southern
slopes of Big Smoky Mountain in eastern Boone County
in the Smoky mountains of East Tennessee. Big Smoky
Mountain itself is a five mile long ridge rising to an ele-
vation of 2,800 feet, or 1,400 feet above the larger creek
valleys of the immediate vicinity. The ridge is only 20
miles from one county seat and 25 from another, but
the isolation of the Little Smoky neighborhood is greater
than the distances suggest. The roads which connect
the neighborhood with the outside world can scarcely
be called a solid link with civilization although conditions have improved in recent years under the Tennessee
Rural Roads Project. Crews of surveyors are a common
sight along the Little River and its tributaries below
Big Smoky Mountain. Every season sees another section "tore up" and completely impassable for months at
a time while gangs of workmen widen and straighten
local roads.

Eventually a network of paved highways will funnel

traffic along Big Smoky Creek and through scenic portions of the mountains to the resort town of Cloudland.
A new section of gravel road opened in 1950 cut the distance between Big Smoky Mountain and Cloudland from
thirteen to six miles. Still, there is no hard-surfaced
road past the mountain, and the road down river toward
the county seat town of Thomasville will probably continue to be narrow and winding because that is the
nature of the river valley. In the other direction around
the eastern end of Big Smoky Mountain there is fairly
easy access down an open valley to another county seat,
Holston, and this is the usual route to the outside for
residents of Little Smoky Ridge.

At present the main highway past Big Smoky Mountain is a narrow, rough, winding and frequently muddy
road that parallels Big Smoky Creek. It is an improvement over the old road which did *not* parallel the creek;
it simply ran through the meandering stream a dozen
times in less than five miles. The old road is now impassable for cars, but there are houses along it and it is
still a foot and mule path. The roads running into Little
Smoky Ridge from the creek are roads by courtesy only.
Each follows a steep and twisting branch of the creek.
They were mere trails in the early days, later widened
to accommodate wagons. Trucks, jeeps and old Fords
can negotiate them in most weather if the owner of the
vehicle has ceased caring what happens to his car.

At least officially the road up Rocky Branch and

down Roaring Branch is a county road and should be maintained at county expense. However, the county is poor. The people of Little Smoky Ridge have little political strength, and there is a tendency on the part of officials to ignore this section of the county. Poor road maintenance is only one form this attitude takes, but it is an obvious one.

County officials are not entirely to blame for the poor roads. One of the things "Aunt" Eliza Bruton and her half-brother Lige Floyd agree on is that they do not want roads near their property. Eliza disapproves of cars and complains about being too near the highway. Lige seems more concerned about the effect on his land of drainage from the road. After repairs had been made on the road a few years ago, one or the other of them dug a ditch which directed run-off down the middle of the road. The natural problem of washouts and gullying on the necessarily steep local roads is bad enough. When an element of human "cussedness" is added, the problem becomes insurmountable.

Muddy, badly washed roads contribute to the isolation of the neighborhood. The Southern Appalachian region has the heaviest rainfall of any major area east of the Pacific coast, which means that unsurfaced roads are frequently impassable. Rainfall is especially heavy in the summer months and again in late winter when downpours may continue for several days at a time. The flow of rivers fluctuates greatly, and floods are common.

Little Smoky Ridge affords a striking example of the increasingly devastating effect of floods on human welfare in the Southern Appalachians. Geologists who surveyed the area between 1900 and 1905 noted that the major creek valleys and lower slopes were cleared and cultivated. The higher slopes were practically untouched by farmers at that time, although lumbermen had already removed the best timber. At that time Big Smoky Creek and its tributaries were clear mountain streams, carrying practically no eroded soil. Floods were only beginning to cause serious damage.

As the years passed, all the original forest was cut, and the steeper slopes came under cultivation. The streams took on a reddish or yellowish-brown color from suspended soil. Damaging floods became more frequent. In the summer of 1938, a cloudburst dropped nearly twelve inches of rain on Big Smoky Mountain. In 1900, the land might have been able to withstand even this unusual amount of water. In 1938 there was little to take up the load.

When anyone in Little Smoky Ridge speaks of "The Flood," he means that terrifying summer night in 1938. As an event from which to date other events, it ranks with the "Big Snow" of 1917. Ask Sula McCoy how old her eldest son is and she does not know exactly, but "he was walking the time of the Flood." Try to learn the exact date of Hettie Brown's death, and "it was just after the Flood." And everyone knows the age of Dan

Johnson's grandson John because he was born on the night of the Flood. The Flood is still a living topic of conversation even with children too young to have witnessed it.

For "Aunt" Eliza Bruton it was the "loneliest and darkest" night of her life. In retrospect she recalls that the whole day was filled with ominous foreboding and she sent for her granddaughter May to stay with her. That night they woke in terror to see flashes of lightning that illuminated the whole mountain and to hear the deafening roar of rushing water and sliding rock. Surely it was the wrath of the Lord loosed to punish the wicked world, and Eliza and May spent the night alternately praying and weeping. Across the hollow, Lige and his family watched a wall of water shoot through the sky and arch high above their heads like a rainbow. It swept his fields clear of crops and soil and rushed on through the house.

On Roaring Branch, Lew Randolph, who has since left the neighborhood, roused his family and barely had time to rush them up the almost perpendicular hillside behind the house. The family huddled together on top of the mountain and looked down. An oil lamp continued to burn inside the house as the waters whirled around, twisting the building first one way and then another until the whole structure tore loose from its foundations and disappeared down the branch.

Farther up Roaring Branch, Will and Jennie McCoy,

living at that time with "Uncle" Eli, were in a house
fully fifty yards back from the normal stream bed. Yet
a sheet of water swept against the house and swung it
half way around. The house might have followed Lew
Randolph's except that Will forced the doors open, and
the family worked for several hours to sweep water and
debris through one door and out the other.

Downstream, the Jones family lost their house, barn
and the year's crops. Jim's sawmill, including a twenty
horsepower boiler, washed away completely. In nearby
neighborhoods two other mills were similarly destroyed.
And in one neighborhood a family of six drowned when
their house was inundated. It was several days before
all the bodies were recovered. Almost everyone in Little
Smoky Ridge possesses a postcard print of the six caskets
at the funeral, a gruesome reminder of the tragedy.

In the whole area about fifty persons were left completely destitute. The National Red Cross sent representatives to head rehabilitation work. The WPA, Health
Department, and local mission also helped.

Relief efforts did not entirely satisfy everyone. The
Red Cross could not pay for losses like an insurance
company yet many thought they should have paid full
value for lost property. There was greater resentment,
however, toward the mission relief. Relations with the
mission have been more lasting and personal and more
often misunderstood than relations with the Red Cross.
Many articles of clothing were sent to the mission for

distribution to flood victims. Pursuing a policy of refusing to give outright charity, the mission sold the
clothing instead of giving it away. At any rate that is
the Little Smoky version of events, and they begrudged
having to pay even a nominal sum for things they knew
had been sent as gifts. Actually, the mission relaxed its
policy considerably during the flood crisis, but the incident still rankles.

In addition to the immediate distress, the flood permanently damaged many acres of land on Big Smoky
Mountain. In a few hours landslides and gullies accomplished a tremendous piece of erosion. Scars are still
visible where rock and soil became heavy with moisture
and broke loose from the mountain side. Stream chan-
nels were deepened by several feet in places, and valleys
along the steep upper branches were stripped to bedrock.

While the cloudburst was a natural phenomenon
beyond any human control, its consequences were
influenced by the cumulative effect of particular
cultural activities, the land use practices of the early
American frontiersman. Those who have viewed the
frontier as the seedbed of later democratic progress
have usually overlooked the fact that the very practices
which secured an independent living for the first settlers made almost certain a state of dependency for
their descendants where the practices were continued.
This is especially apparent in the mountainous portions

of the Southern Appalachian region which was America's first western frontier.

For most of the Southern Appalachian region early conditions changed rapidly. Many activities were as fleeting as the wilderness which fostered them. Dense forests, hostile Indians and isolation gave way to settled agriculture, industrial development and the growth of towns and cities. In some places, however, wilderness conditions continued and the older activities remained alive.

Thus, although Little Smoky Ridge was settled a century or more after the initial opening of the region, its first inhabitants were following customs little different from their Colonial ancestors. The appearance of Jim Floyd in the neighborhood, shotgun in hand, seeking new land for his growing family, is reminiscent of earlier pioneer men who preceded their families into the western country to "spy out the land," make the first clearing and put in the first crop. The search for land was often incidental to a hunting trip as it was for that intrepid Tennesseean Davy Crockett, who might almost be speaking for Jim Floyd:

We turned in and cleared a field, and planted our corn, but it was so late in the spring, we had no time to make rails, and therefore, we put no fence around the field. There was no stock, however, nor any thing else to disturb our corn, except the wild varments, and the old serpent himself, with a fence to help him, couldn't keep them out. I made enough corn to do me, and during the

spring I killed ten bears, and a great abundance of deer.
... Having laid by my crap [sic], I went home, which
was a distance of about a hundred and fifty miles.[1]

As in earlier times, so in Little Smoky Ridge in the
1870s, land clearing and house building were the first
order of business for a man establishing himself in a new
neighborhood. Jim Floyd cut pine logs for his first house
and prepared oak planks for the door. Neighbors helped
him raise and notch the logs in one day, and he and his
family completed the one room, windowless house at
their leisure, including a fireplace so long that all seven-
teen members of the family could sit in front of it.

Neighbors also helped him clear land that year and in
later years, for Jim "was a great one to clear a little
farther up the mountain every year." Present day residents recall these "log rollings":

The first settlers here near slaughtered the timber. The
man who owned the field would clear off the brush and
then have a log rolling to pile and burn the logs. Every-
body would come to start piling logs from the top or
one end of the field, cutting green trees and all to get
the shade off the land. The old people believed in raking
over the whole land and burning all the brush and logs.
All they thought was to clear. They didn't know they
were wasting more than they were making. They didn't
know what was coming. They didn't know there'd be
a tannery where they could have sold the bark.

Such neighborhood "workings" are now a thing of the
past:

There are no more log rollings in this country now. It finally got so a man just asked three or four to help with a job. Back just after the [Civil] War you had to have workings to open up the land and make anything. You wouldn't even pretend to clear anything without a working because there was big heavy timber then.

The increasing poverty of the neighborhood through the years also helped to lessen the importance of neighborhood work parties. When the good timber had been destroyed "people just built any kind of house to get along with." Jim Floyd's granddaughter Eliza and her husband decided against holding a working when they built a house forty years ago because "we couldn't afford to kill all them chickens and make all them dumplings for everyone." The idea remained but not the means to realize it.

With less and less chance to achieve the pioneer goals, the Ridge continued to be essentially a frontier neighborhood well into the present century. It was frontier in the sense of being on the outer fringe, or perhaps more accurately, in the backwater of settlement. It was frontier also in continuing to consist of family units living mainly by crude subsistence farming combined with hunting.

Generations of frontier land use have placed the present population in a cultural trap on land beyond repair. No amount of cover crops or fertilizers is likely to restore production; and heavy rains on bare, steep slopes further aggravate the erosion problem.

All this suggests that there is an important relation between human activities and nature in the neighborhood. Local topography, climate, and traditional ways of adjusting to the natural environment help to explain the present conditions. A knowledge of position relative to the whole Southern Appalachian region is also basic to an understanding of limiting factors in the development and present position of remote settlements like Little Smoky Ridge.

Physiographically, the Southern Appalachian region includes three distinct provinces, the Blue Ridge and Smoky Mountains on the east, the Appalachian plateaus on the west, and the great Appalachian valleys in the middle. The whole region covers about 110,000 square miles in more than 200 counties of Maryland, Virginia, West Virginia, eastern Kentucky, eastern Tennessee, western North Carolina, northwestern South Carolina, northern Georgia, and northeastern Alabama.[2] The region is 650 miles long from northeast to southwest and averages 170 miles in width. It is a landlocked area of relatively high altitudes between the Piedmont Plateau on the east and south and the Mississippi Valley on the west. The region's mountains, valleys and dissected plateaus distinguish it from the surrounding lowlands.

The great central Appalachian Valley had special significance in the early settlement and subsequent development of the region. High mountain ranges flank its eastern border and the lower Cumberlands rise gradually along its western edge. The main lines of transportation and communication through the region have always been along the northeast to southwest axis of the central valley from Maryland to Alabama.

Lines of communication and the distribution of land that could be profitably cultivated have had a great effect on human development in this region. In the Southern Appalachians, American civilization expanded along the rivers and streams of a wilderness frontier. It grew and flourished as the frontier filled with people who established an agricultural and commercial economy. Trading centers developed along the principal transportation lines. But between the valleys and in the inaccessible parts of the mountain and plateau provinces progress did not keep pace with the valley sections.

The height, swift drainage and ruggedness of the whole Blue Ridge and Smoky Mountain province contrasts with the relative flatness, fertility and easy communication of the valley province. There are also important differences within the mountain province itself. Everywhere in the mountains there are sections of lower and smoother land that can be placed under profitable cultivation, but they are scattered across the map in a patchwork arrangement along stream valleys and in basins and "coves." These patches range in size from narrow strips along small creeks to the Asheville Basin which covers parts of three counties in western North Carolina. But they step down in a series of unconnected benches from the higher valleys to the main valley floors.

Population has always been greatest in the major valleys and in the larger basins and coves. In general cultivable lands are smaller farther upstream and population is correspondingly sparser. Large farms are possible and profitable only where the land is good and road building does not present a major engineering problem. The higher valleys and coves of the Smoky Mountains were virtually isolated from each other and from larger centers until the road building projects of the past fifteen to twenty years. Population is still sparsest on the steep-sided unprofitable ridges. And Little Smoky Ridge is such a settlement.

In the soils as in the topography there is a contrast between the valleys and the ridges.[3] The limestone-based valleys and the limestone pockets scattered through the mountains contain fertile, although often shallow, soil. The soils of the mountain ridges are another story. The sandstones, quartzites and conglomerates of the ridge lands yield sandy or stony soils of low fertility. Bedrock occurs near the surface, and steep slopes add to the difficulty of cultivation and increase the problem of erosion.

Little Smoky Ridge has typical ridge soils on steep slopes. According to TVA soil surveys in the neighborhood only a few acres on the lower part of Roaring Branch should ever be used for anything but pasture or woodland. It may be scientifically sound to classify these lands as unfit for crops, but it is pretty futile. Fields of corn, tobacco and beans still climb the steep hillsides. Some lands in the vicinity have been taken out of cultivation by being added to the Great Smoky Mountains National Park, thus creating human problems for displaced persons while solving other problems.

Destruction of forest cover has also added to the problem of maintaining even a minimum population on the ridges of the region. Most of the originally extensive forests have been cut over. The cutting went on for more than a century under the frontier system of clearing new lands as old ones lost their fertility. The later cutting by lumbermen in the latter part of the nineteenth and early twentieth century merely continued and hastened a process long under way. The present inhabitants of Little Smoky Ridge may be thought of as representing a final stage in a long period of successive clearing, exhaustion, and abandonment of lands farther and farther up the sides of the mountains.

CHAPTER THREE

The Path of Settlement

TOPOGRAPHIC FEATURES DETERMINED THE HISTORIC paths of settlement and thus the present distribution of population in the Southern Appalachians. The broad river valleys were first to be settled. Then settlement turned along the creeks and branches. The remote Smoky Mountain ridges were last to be settled in a general pattern which began in the Colonial period and continued in some places well into the twentieth century.

On the Tennessee side of the Smoky Mountains in Boone County, settlement moved up the Big and Little rivers, on up Big Smoky and Lusty creeks, and finally up Roaring, Rocky and Morgan branches of Little Smoky Ridge. First into the coves and wider valleys, then into the narrower valleys, and finally up the slopes of the ridges. It was 1860 before Dan Johnson's father, arriving on one of the lower branches, swapped a "hog rifle" for 150 acres of land from the original owner. He immediately sold a small parcel of land to another settler, built a double log house for his family, and went off to fight in the Civil War.

It was another decade or so before Eliza Bruton's grandfather, Jim Floyd, rode over from Judson County on his "jack" and entered a claim for 600 acres on Rocky Branch in the upper part of Little Smoky Ridge. In his lifetime he deeded parts of his land to three daughters and two sons.

The father of Elmer Morgan and Jennie McCoy arrived just before the end of the nineteenth century to become the second settler on what is now called Morgan Branch. He purchased 200 acres from the original owner for a sum of about fifty dollars and erected a double log house on the present site of Will McCoy's somewhat smaller log house.

None of the first settlers on the Ridge had come any great distance. They arrived from nearby counties in East Tennessee, or from North or South Carolina. They could already count several generations in mountain settlements relatively isolated from larger communities in the Appalachian Valley province or the Piedmont of the Carolinas. They were descendants of hunters and small farmers who had intermarried to a slight extent with Indian inhabitants of the region.

Since their arrival in Little Smoky Ridge there has been much dividing and swapping of land until present day descendants have tracts of about forty acres instead of the original 100 to 600 acre tracts. Many log and frame houses have been built, remodeled, torn down or sometimes moved "log by log" from one site to another since the early days.

The broad picture of settlement is clear. The settlers in the Smoky Mountains were simply part of the general movement which began to fill the country west of the Appalachian divide in the late eighteenth and early nineteenth century. However, the specific details are difficult to reconstruct. Historians have dealt at length with the peopling of the larger Appalachian valleys, but they have lacked interest and information for considering the more remote settlements.

The earliest settlers in the region certainly chose the better lands along the large rivers, and those especially interested in commercial ventures continued to seek the fertile valleys and the main lines of access to markets. Yet many who were moving west in the decades following the Revolutionary War were not primarily commercial in their outlook. Their goal was land enough to support a family, good springs, a supply of wild game, and timber and stone for building. Mountain coves and valleys, once they were discovered at all, proved as attractive to this type of settler as the valley province. Certainly there were settlers in the lower valleys around Big Smoky Mountain by the end of the eighteenth century at a time when Indians still constituted a threat in the area. But the population remained scattered, and there were no good roads into this part of the mountains before 1900, although there had been intermittent travel and settlement for more than a century.

The original movement into the Southern Appalachian region consisted of at least four partially overlapping stages.[1] British settlement through the Colonial period had been largely in the Tidewater region. The first movement was coastwise and then up the Atlantic rivers to the fall line. The second movement was from east to west into sections of the Piedmont between the Tidewater and Appalachian regions. By the third stage settlement had penetrated to the headwaters of rivers in the Appalachian valleys and was proceeding from northeast to southwest along the natural line of these valleys. Finally, transmontane routes across the Appalachian divide into the lower Mississippi Valley came into greater use.

The first important westward movement beyond the fall line began about 1720 along rivers which could be easily followed from South Carolina to the Blue Ridge country. Movement from the coast into central Virginia was also relatively easy, and the Valley of Virginia began to fill between 1730 and 1750. As early as 1740, a few had crossed the low divides into the Piedmont section of North Carolina. From all these settlements hunters, traders and surveyors were penetrating far into Tennessee and Kentucky. Their accounts stirred land speculators and prospective settlers to push farther west until by 1770:

Masses of population were upon the western boundary of all the middle and southern colonies, ready and impatient for the occupancy of new lands in the wilderness. They knew the avenues by which they could be reached, and had spread among their countrymen enchanting accounts of their value and beauty. Another circumstance hastened the more perfect exploration and future settlement of the western country. It was the bounty given in these very lands, by several of the provinces with the approbation of the crown, to the officers and soldiers who had served in the British army, in the wars with the French and their Indian allies. These, with the script and miltary warrants in their hands, and accompanied by hundreds of surveyors and agents, were constantly employed in selecting and locating their respective claims.[2]

Once the westward movement was on in earnest, Crown and colonies alike treated the Proclamation of 1763, reserving "to the Indians . . . for the present" all the lands from the Alleghenies to the Mississippi River, as a dead letter. Only the exceptionally powerful Cherokee tribe was able to block the path of settlement into much of their territory for a few more decades. They continued to hold large parts of the Tennessee Valley for many years. Settlers were unable to penetrate as far south as the Little Tennessee before 1798, and the Hiwassee District farther south was held by the Indians until 1819.

For several decades after the Revolution, all the main arteries of travel and trade to the developing western

regions of the new republic continued to cross the
Southern Appalachian region. By 1820, however, most
of the western traffic had turned along the Ohio River
into the Northwest Territory. Thereafter, local movements continued within the Southern Appalachian
region, but there were no more large influxes of population from other regions.

While the Valley province remained in touch with
other parts of the country and participated in national
developments, the mountains became effectively isolated from the main stream of rising American civilization until the Civil War again brought them into
contact with national events. The old pattern of settlement repeated itself deeper and deeper into the mountains under conditions favoring the development of a
folk society. Ways that disappeared rapidly on other
frontiers here became true folkways sanctioned by tradition and unchallenged by any alternative set of customs or values.

This period of isolation established the Southern Appalachian culture with its numerous diffuse, kinship-
centered neighborhood societies. It also, in a sense, set
the stage for the ultimate breakdown of the culture.
Given the particular cultural tradition (the pioneer
farming techniques coupled with a willingness to move
from one homestead site to another as opposed to any
strong desire to put down roots in one location) it was
only a question of time and reaching the limits of avail-

able land for economic deterioration to begin. (See Chapter Eight)

Pursuing this course, most of the pioneers to the Tennessee side of the Smoky Mountains entered the area by rough trails up the valleys and through gaps in the main ranges. They came from the valleys of Virginia and East Tennessee, from the North Carolina Piedmont through Swannanoa or Hickory Nut gaps, or through Cashiers Valley from South Carolina, taking several generations to reach the limits of expansion.

Early land policies in this part of the mountains changed frequently, and surveys were often inaccurate.[3] Entries were made haphazardly if at all, and entries made in the land offices of Virginia, Franklin, and North Carolina, not to mention private purchases from Indians, overlapped. Possession has frequently assumed more than the usual "nine points of the law," and "squatter's rights" usually go unchallenged even today in the poorer sections of the mountains.

The present inhabitants of Little Smoky Ridge live on land which they own, with or without clear title, or "rent" on vaguely defined terms.[4] The majority occupy land acquired through inheritance and on which they pay taxes more or less regularly. Often the head of the family claims ownership, but his children may pay some of the taxes or in other ways compensate for the use of land they will eventually inherit.

In theory land is divided equally among a man's children, daughters as well as sons. In the past, practice seems to have conformed closely to theory. At present it frequently happens that some members of a family have left the neighborhood. In such cases the remaining members divide the land and pay the others only if there is a demand for settlement.

For a largely land-owning population, the people in Little Smoky Ridge are surprisingly mobile. Families move in and out of local houses or to other neighborhoods, only to reappear in their old homes in a year or two. Present mobility might be explained in terms of discouraging yields from worn out land and the perennial hope of bettering the situation by a move, but this may be only a partial explanation. Family histories indicate that frequent moves within a radius of two or three counties have been common for several generations. Eliza Bruton, for example, has lived in seven different houses on her grandfather's orginal 600 acres and, in addition, has lived in other neighborhoods in three different counties. Each of her eleven children, who appeared about two years apart, was born in a different house.

Most of the moves are over relatively short distances to similar mountain neighborhoods although a few families have moved to small towns nearby or even outside the region. Changing residence is not the complex matter it is for urbanites. The decision to move is not made quickly, for there is no urgency. The idea seems to creep into the daily talk. Perhaps it is never far beneath the surface. Gradually reasons for a change accumulate and are discussed. The roof leaks, "that fireplace never did draw right," the kitchen is too hot or too cold, and the like, are all sufficient reasons for contemplating a move. The advantages and disadvantages of all the vacant houses for miles around are considered. Finally a place is chosen. If the house happens to belong to someone with whom the family can claim kinship, arrangements are extremely informal. Even if the owner is not a relative, there is rarely any sort of formal agreement. The owner may retain some of the land for his own use or the family may agree to work the land "on halves"; but the owner exercises little control over the kind of crops to be raised.

So long as the land in Little Smoky Ridge continues to have little value, ownership based on vague titles and renting on an informal basis is satisfactory. Residents of some adjacent neighborhoods, however, experienced the unhappy outcome of such non-legal arrangements when land they felt they owned suddenly acquired a new value about 25 years ago as a potential part of the Great Smoky Mountains National Park.

Whatever benefits the Park has brought to the region as a whole, many of the dispossessed local people remain bitter. The trouble began when the State of Tennessee, aided by Rockefeller money, authorized the purchase of several large tracts owned by lumber companies and of from 1,100 to 1,500 small tracts owned by individuals.

The negotiations led to accusations that owners were being unduly threatened and that certain commissioners were party to private real estate deals that cheated both the landowners and the State.

After the Federal Government entered the picture, the acquisition of land by purchase, arbitration and through the courts continued. About 400 families were granted life-time leases to remain in their homes on Park land. Perhaps 600 families left the Park area, and much was done to find them new homes. However, a fictional (?) account from a neighboring county suggests another side:

The Drennons had that hundred acres of land that was theirn. At least it always had been theirn. Other folks around there close to them had been having to sell their land to the Smoky Mountain Park folks so the Government could have it for big bugs to come and look at, and so they could kill off all the deer that folks around here liked to keep safe so we could have them to look at. Of course, if a body wouldn't sell his land the Government just took it whether or no. And claimed they got folks some other good place to live.

.   .   .   .

Erve told him, "Grandpa had a deed for it and we hain't never had it changed to our names. Pa never did have it changed to hisn. It come down to Pa from Grandpa Drennon, of course. Then it come down to me and Everett from Pa."[5]

To this day people along Big Smoky Creek and in Little Smoky Ridge speak of prosperous times and big community affairs "before the Government run our people off." There are complaints that the government took the best land, though soil and land use maps do not bear this out. The sentiment against the Park follows a common local attitude of resentment toward outside interference, but the population loss occasioned by Park purchases perhaps did indirectly affect the welfare of the remaining families whose political strength in the county has remained slight. Programs for the extension of good roads, electricity and other services have largely by-passed this part of the county until very recently.

The mountain slopes and ridges of the area have always been off the main path of commercial and industrial development. If anything, they became more isolated because of land purchases for the Park. The total effect of geographic and historical factors has contributed to the retention in Little Smoky Ridge and similar neighborhoods of an economic pattern first established on the early American frontier.

CHAPTER FOUR

A Frontier Economy and Some Twentieth Century Results

LITTLE SMOKY RIDGE STANDS AS A TWENTIETH CEN-
tury illustration of the persistence of a frontier type of
social organization and value system in an environment
no longer suited to either. Nowhere is this more apparent
than in the economic activities of neighborhood families
who continue a tradition of patch farming and hunting
on land that can no longer support these occupations.

Self-sufficiency, which was a keynote of pioneer economy, remains a value in Little Smoky Ridge, but for
small mountain farms it is a value impossible of achievement. Families in the past could and did supply most of
their wants from materials in the wilderness at hand.
Today not a single family in the neighborhood can maintain itself solely from the products of the land. As suggested earlier, the very customs which made for survival in a virgin wilderness became self-defeating in the
cul-de-sac of the mountains.

The cultural similarity between ridge settlements like

Little Smoky Ridge and the early frontier could easily be overstated, but there is much evidence to support Turner's general thesis that the wilderness mastered the colonist and transformed him from the diversity of his European backgrounds to something new and characteristically American.[1] Still, differences of time and space and European provenience are clearly reflected in regional variations that arose in American culture. It is therefore necessary to examine the special variant of frontier society and culture that shaped the modern Little Smoky Ridges of the Southern Appalachians.

There was considerable local variation in cultural bias even from the start. The Southern Appalachian region as a whole offers a variety of resources and through the centuries has supported a number of types of human occupation, the result of varying combinations of geographic, social, and cultural features. White settlers brought several different patterns of land use to the region. And the first English, Scotch, Scotch-Irish, French and German pioneers reacted differently to the new conditions according to their past cultural experiences.[2]

Many of the British, who were most numerous in the early population, brought virtually no agricultural skills to their new environment. Farming and hunting were a necessity forced on them by circumstance, and the economic complex they adopted was derived almost en-

tirely from the aboriginal Indian population. Cultural
differences soon appeared, however, between British
settlers in the valley communities and those who spread
into the mountains. Even at first, the contrast probably reflected some diversity of background and interests, although other factors of communication, availability of cultivable land, and position relative to large
towns were at least equally important in distributing
the population.

The particular cultural ways still present in Little
Smoky Ridge are those of the British pioneer fringe that
pushed through the valleys of Pennsylvania and Virginia
and back into the Piedmont section of the Carolinas or
that moved directly from the coast into the back country of North and South Carolina and from there into
the mountains. The great mass of these emigrants from
more settled regions brought little in the way of material
wealth or capital with them. They came by the tens of
thousands toward the end of the Colonial period and immediately following the Revolution.

This was primarily a movement of humble folk, of families hopefully seeking a cheaper, better, and freer life
than they had hitherto known. Among them existed a
marked disparity of wealth. Poverty was the common
badge of the majority of Ulsterites, although here and
there a man of property could be found. Their nearest
rivals were the Highland Scots, who came late in the period. I am inclined to think that despite the fact that
most of the Palatines and Swiss were also poor, there

was a larger number who possessed at least a little property than among the other groups. At any rate it is clear that by their cautiousness in selection of land and care in their husbandry, by their willingness to work hard, and by sharing tools and effects with one another, they seemed from the first to make a better life of it than the Scotch-Irish. Among the westward-moving colonials the widest range existed, from abject poverty to considerable wealth in land and slaves. A pair of horses or yoke of oxen, a small wagonload of household and farm effects, plus some cattle, hogs, and poultry made up all the capital of the average family.[3]

There were hunters, livestock raisers and both subsistence and commercial farmers among the emigrants, but for several decades hunting with a little patch farming and a few head of stock loomed large in the region's economy. As population increased and a settled agricultural economy became established, the hunters, herders and patch farmers moved on into newer Western territories or back into the mountains and piney woods of the South.[4] It is the ways of this element that are most apparent in Little Smoky Ridge, although game and livestock have ceased to have much economic importance. It is mainly the attitudes that remain, especially as masculine virtues, though none of the local men could hope to express values in the grand manner of a Davy Crockett, who could boast:

I gathered my corn, and then set out for my Fall's hunt. This was in the last of October, 1822. I found bear very plenty, and, indeed, all sorts of game and wild varments, except buffalo. There was none of them. I hunted on till Christmas, having supplied my family very well all along with wild meat, at which time my powder gave out; and I had none either to fire Christmas guns which is very common in that country, or to hunt with.[5]

The frontiersman has apparently always represented more than an occupational type. Early descriptions of his special dress, rough amusements and propensity for leaving his crops untended or in the hands of his women-folk provide insight into some of the potent symbolism which even now keeps men in Little Smoky Ridge from modifying their behavior to conform to twentieth century realities. The leather hunting shirt, leggings, moccasins and coonskin cap were practical, but they were also symbolic of masculinity and a special way of life.

Many of the early hunters changed readily enough to livestock raising and more concern with farming as the region became more settled. Yet in all periods there has been a class, somewhat shifting in its composition, that has kept to the outer fringe of settlement, clinging to hunting supplemented by a little farming. They have maintained a continuity of tradition from frontier to Little Smoky Ridge.

While hunting no longer constitutes a major economic pursuit, all of the men and most boys in Little Smoky possess shotguns or rifles which they use expertly. A man rarely leaves the house without his gun, although

the occasional squirrel he brings home hardly merits such
constant readiness. Nor is the gun really needed for
protection; it is simply part of the "proper" costume
for males, like the hat which is worn indoors and out at
all times.

Actually, hunting has only recently declined as an important source of meat. At least one middle-aged man
in the neighborhood has a reputation as a great bear
hunter. With the present laws for protecting bears he
is unable openly to maintain his reputation, but probably most of the present residents know the taste of
bear meat. Certainly all of them frequently have
smaller game, though not in the quantity remembered
by the older generation whose parents dried and cured
wild meat for winter use.

Spending less time at hunting, however, has not meant
that the men spend noticeably more time at farming.
Their attitude toward farming remains that of the pioneer who was more woodsman than agriculturalist and
who had no special love for tilling the soil. Even with
increased reliance on cash crops, the general approach
suggests the rather casual manner with which the men
have always turned to whatever occupation presented
itself when the need for money became especially pressing. If anything, the indifference toward farming has
increased as the hope for making a living on steep, worn-
out fields has decreased and as new fields are no longer
readily available.

Conditions have changed from the time when a man could support his family from the forests and clear enough land every two or three years to supply corn, potatoes and whatever else he chose to plant. With successive divisions of property and loss of soil fertility, cultivable land is scarce even by local standards of cultivability.

The significance of cultural factors in creating modern conditions can be shown by comparing Little Smoky Ridge with mountain settlements having a different cultural background. There are equally isolated ridge settlements that have continued to provide an adequate subsistence through the same years that Little Smoky was becoming increasingly impoverished. The remote Swiss colony of Gruetli, Tennessee, in the rugged Cumberland Plateau provides a striking example.[6]

Gruetli was settled in almost exactly the same period as Little Smoky Ridge, 1869 to 1875. Its population of eighteen families in 1943 compares roughly with the eighteen to twenty households of Little Smoky Ridge in 1949 and 1950. There the similarities stop, for Gruetli was a planned agricultural community while Little Smoky just "happened." Plans for Gruetli included a road system, general store, post office and other community services for the families who settled on tracts of about 100 acres each. (Tracts in Little Smoky Ridge originally ranged from 100 to 600 acres each.)

The Swiss, mainly from the peasant and lower middle

class, developed farming as their main occupation although a few were artisans in masonry, coopery, carpentry or cabinet making. Their major asset in developing the none too promising land of Grundy County was their knowledge of intensive agriculture coupled with a love and respect for the land. They used soil and forests with care, clearing only a few acres for crops while preserving their forest land. They insured high crop yields over many years by the use of grasses, clovers, manure, crop rotation and lime.

The unplanned settlement of Little Smoky Ridge by individualistic hunter-farmers represents the opposite extreme. Its creators loved the mountains but not the soil. Lacking attachment to any particular spot they were prepared to move on when necessary. They had no knowledge of intensive agriculture. Instead, they were committed to the destructive extensive methods of their forebears, and these could be successful only so long as the supply of new land was unlimited. The result is the cultural blind alley in which they today find themselves.

Bound by tradition, no one in the neighborhood considers farming a worthy year round profession for a real man. There is little else to do, but slack seasons continue to be periods for leisure and non-farm activities. Even in the busiest part of the farm year, attention to crops is not a continuous concern.

It is generally recognized in the neighborhood that the land is less productive than it used to be. Some realize that traditional farming practices have done much to destroy fertility, but they also have other explanations. The Government is blamed because it took the good land and forced displaced families to cultivate land they knew should not be cropped every year. A few, expressing family cleavages, blame their neighbors for ruining the land with tobacco while maintaining that their own tobacco land is properly cared for. Still others turn to the supernatural and explain crop failure and soil conditions by "the wickedness of the people" or "God's punishment."

Today as in the past crop acreages vary from year to year and from person to person with no long range planning for land use. A man "takes a notion" to put a particular hillside into corn, or beans, or something else. Most families have less than fifteen acres under cultivation. Thirty acres is the most any family has in crops and the least is less than five acres. The principal crops are those common to most of the mountain counties of Tennessee—corn, beans, tobacco, Irish and sweet potatoes, cabbage, and a variety of garden vegetables according to individual taste.

Increased reliance on cash crops has been a feature of the past generation as the neighborhood has found it necessary to participate more fully in the general American economy. About half the local farms produce either tobacco or beans, or both, for market. None of these are large scale operations, however, and it is im-

possible to state the actual value of cash crops as a source
of income. There is no bookkeeping and a tendency to
exaggerate, or to forget production costs, also makes
evaluation difficult. When a man boasts that he made
three or four hundred dollars on his beans or tobacco,
closer investigation usually reveals that he has not
counted the cost of seeds, fertilizer, labor, or transportation to market.

Whatever the actual net income, many potential
profits are lost under the current system of handling
and marketing produce. Marketing is done individually
and erratically like so many other activities. Through
July and August, for example, local men take their
beans to White City whenever they have a truckload,
when they can borrow or rent a truck if they do not
own one, or when other matters do not seem more pressing. Since the bean market fluctuates considerably, the
price that day may be anything from fifty cents to four
dollars per bushel. Profits from tobacco are equally irregular and are often further reduced when portions of
the crop are ruined by excessive dampness or blight before the warehouses open in the late fall.

Present marketing habits are obviously not geared to
a modern commercial economy. Rather, they continue
an earlier pattern which took men from home at irregular intervals for indefinite lengths of time to trans-
port livestock, hides, whiskey and other products of the
frontier to the large market centers of the Old South.

They returned with salt, tools, ammunition, household utensils and whatever little luxuries they could afford. Today's trips are more frequent and of shorter duration, but one is tempted to think of the cheap hotels where the men stay in White City as the modern equivalent of the cattle "stands" of another century.

At first of course most of the back mountain settlements had to supply the greater part of their needs locally. Each family was largely self-sufficient, although there were at least part-time specialists in some occupations. Probably the first full-time specialists in most sections were millers. Small grist mills were ubiquitous, and many of them doubled as sawmills. Itinerant peddlers also visited even the more remote communities with some manufactured goods. And country stores operated in most areas to supply "extras" that could not be produced locally, thus bringing selected portions of the outside world into the mountains.

Life has continued in this manner for folk in Little Smoky Ridge for as many generations as they can remember. The men market crops and do some shopping in White City and smaller trade centers. Three nearby grist mills grind local corn into meal, and as many sawmills process the small amounts of local timber. Several country stores offer more variety than in the past at higher prices in a time when the people have less with which to pay than their grandparents or great grandparents. For a major economic fact in the neighborhood history has been an increasing need for greater production and larger income with decreasing opportunities for achieving them. Small mountain farms are not especially profitable under the best of agricultural practices. The use of light plows, runnered sleds, hand labor and a tendency to let the crops "make themselves," along with the casual marketing habits combine with steep, sterile fields to defeat the local farmer in any competition for market profits.

Farming cannot save the economy, and resources for non-farm income are slight. There have been periods in the past when lumbering offered considerable opportunity. At present the principal source of extra income is from the manufacture and sale of illegal corn whiskey.

Homemade whiskey has always functioned importantly in the social life of neighborhood men. Drinking is one of the many symbols of masculinity of the old frontiersman, and all but four or five of the adult men of Little Smoky Ridge are heavy drinkers. Younger boys also assert their developing manhood by joining the drinking bouts, and at least one ten year old occasionally peddles whiskey at school.

Whiskey making did not become a major source of income, however, until the era of national prohibition. Since most counties in East Tennessee have remained legally "dry," the market has continued. At present the business is well organized through several counties with most of the profits going to persons outside the immediate vicinity. Still, local producers and distributors can make more money than they are accustomed to getting from other activities. Moreover, setting up and watching stills and making the trip to Mill Town with the finished product suit local work habits better than more regulated jobs.

At least fifteen men of the neighborhood derive some income from liquor. Two or three direct fairly large scale operations for which they provide the capital. Others are "watchers" who actually run the stills and stand guard to ward off intruders. The few not actually engaged in the business share the general opinion that a man has a right to make whiskey and do with it what he pleases. By and large county officials ignore Little Smoky Ridge in this activity just as in other matters, although several local men have served short prison terms. Federal agents are considerably more effective and therefore more feared than constables and sheriffs. It is the younger men, who do the final transporting between the Ridge and Mill Town for wider distribution, who are most likely to be apprehended. A fairly elaborate system of lookout and dynamite signals is used during this part of the operation, and any strange car is "tailed" through Mill Town. But the trip is hazardous for other reasons, too. Three major accidents in a single month in 1949 involved cars speeding over the narrow, winding road to dispose of bootleg whiskey.

For obvious reasons it is impossible to ascertain how

much income a family derives from its moonshining activities. When all the costs of production and transportation are considered, it is doubtful whether even the biggest operators clear more than a few dollars on a "run." It is only in the light of other alternatives that the business appeals as a quick way to make money since a batch of whiskey can be made and sold in about one month.

The few other local opportunities to earn money are not fully exploited. Owners of larger farms and orchards in the lower valleys complain that they cannot get all the labor they need. One operator for a while offered ten cents more per hour than the usual rate but soon lost the men he attracted with this inducement because he was "too particular."

In recent years perhaps half a dozen men from the Ridge have worked intermittently on road projects in the area. Men also go occasionally to the county seats or White City or even to industrial centers outside the region to "find a piece of work." They may be away for several weeks or months at a time. For some in every generation such absences become permanent. For most, Little Smoky Ridge continues to be "home," and they return frequently.

The whole subject of adjustment to contemporary American civilization will be considered in Chapters Nine and Ten, but several factors operating to make ventures into the outside labor market unsuccessful may be mentioned here. In the first place, few of the men have any marketable skills or trades. As unskilled labor they occupy the lowest rungs of the industrial ladder and are among the first to be fired in times of depression or recession. Lack of reading ability is also a considerable handicap to many who are unable to decipher the numerous signs that are so much a part of urban and industrial life.

Perhaps more important than near-illiteracy and lack of technical skills are certain personal characteristics that derive from childhood experiences within the traditional family system. The men do not care for steady jobs. They feel no special pressure to acquire money and material possessions as status symbols. In addition, their sense of personal independence frequently finds expression as resentment of being bossed. They are easily angered at real or fancied attacks on their freedom to come and go, work or not, as they please. A clock-regulated industrial system is totally foreign to all their training, and many give up in disgust to return to the (for them) more comfortable ways of Little Smoky Ridge.

No picture of the twentieth century results of the frontier economy would be complete without reference to welfare agencies and charitable organizations. For five households in the neighborhood monthly welfare checks provide the surest and largest single source of income. In most other households welfare money for emergency purposes is important at times. All families also receive gifts of clothing and other supplies from the Russell Cove Mission either occasionally or chronically.

It is interesting to see how accepting welfare and charity has been fitted into local values of pride and independence. It is clear that acquiring money from a welfare agency is not in itself considered degrading. Indeed accepting welfare money seems almost as legitimate as earning it by some other method. As one woman puts it, "It's the good Lord taking care of me because I've worked hard all my life and prayed to Him." Knowledge that a neighbor is receiving welfare checks is more apt to elicit envy than pity or condemnation. It is the families along Big Smoky Creek and the other more favored parts of the county who come closer to reflecting middle class American values. They are the ones who complain of working hard to pay taxes that support the folks back on the mountain who are too lazy to work.

While public welfare from an impersonal agency is accepted as a legitimate source of income, "charity" is defined differently and treated disdainfully by all but the John Bruton family. Some of the Russell Cove missionaries have missed the significance of this distinction, thereby increasing the gulf between themselves and those they sought to serve. Not appreciating neighborhood values, the missionary feels hurt when his "gifts" fail to bring grateful thanks from recipients who do not wish to be objects of charity.

The relations between the Mission and Little Smoky

Ridge are confusing to all participants because of their ambiguity. On one hand, the Mission is as formal and impersonal an agency as the Department of Public Welfare. Most of the time its formal functions of providing school, medical and religious facilities seem to be understood. Its legitimacy in these fields is generally accepted even by those who have no special desire for such services. Its role as a charitable institution for relieving immediate economic distress is also accepted, at least part of the time by part of the population.

On the other hand, relations with the Mission are always more or less personal. Its workers are known and liked or disliked as personalities. When gifts are given or services performed at this interpersonal, informal level, pride demands that the recipient ask, "How much do I owe you?" For small services no one really expects a price to be named. For larger ones a person does expect to pay, by a return gift or favor if not in cash. Any hint of inequality between donor and recipient is quickly sensed and resented.

Attitudes toward the Mission are further colored by generalized feelings toward "foreigners," or outsiders. It was outsiders who established the original center at Russell Cove and spread their evangelical work to surrounding neighborhoods. Although the Mission school is now incorporated into the county system and staffed by county teachers, the rest of the Mission remains "outside" after more than thirty years.

CHAPTER FIVE

First Contacts with the Outside

THE RETENTION OF A FRONTIER TRADITION PARTIALLY explains present conditions in Little Smoky Ridge and similar neighborhoods. Settlement along mountain ridges in small, atomistic neighborhoods isolated from each other and cut off from growing population centers encouraged crystallization of a folk culture oriented toward preserving the ways of the past. On the other hand, the very nature of the relationships that finally developed with representatives of the outside world has also been instrumental in setting the conservatism and general unreceptiveness to innovation of these remote, sparsely populated sections of the mountains. Outsiders have more often exploited than enriched the region in the past and have left the people more stranded, impoverished, less self-sufficient, and in a poorer position to meet later contacts.

By the time outside influence began making itself felt in the latter half of the nineteenth century, the mountain and plateau provinces of the Southern Appalachian region had been relatively isolated for two, three, or more generations. Before 1820, the region had been part of the first great thrust of American civilization into the lands west of the Appalachian divide, and all major routes flowed into or through the region. When the tide of American expansion turned north and west after that date, the whole South to some degree and the Southern mountains to a large degree became separated from the rest of the country. No longer receiving thousands of immigrants each year, the population grew only by natural increase.

Families continued to shift and spread within the mountains, but parts of the region actually lost population despite a high rate of natural increase because large numbers were leaving to seek lands still farther to the south and west. Even where population was increasing, the rate of gain was considerably less than the national average. East Tennessee, for example, reached a low point in population increase relative to the rest of the state in 1870.[1] Since then its growth has accelerated, but the demographic fact of its slow increase cannot be overlooked in accounting for its underdevelopment in other respects. The related fact that the mountain counties could not support a large population at an adequate economic level is equally important.

During the years of isolation social and cultural differences multiplied between those who stayed in the mountains and those whose fortunes remained joined to the larger national culture. Cities, trade, agriculture, and industry grew rapidly into a vast commercially oriented civilization on the "outside" while the pace and activities of life remained substantially unchanged back in the mountains.

When outside forces finally found their way into the mountain world, they came in the form of bitter civil war followed in a few years by ruinous exploitation of timber and mineral resources. The forces did not arrive in all parts of the mountains at once, nor did they come in a single guise. The effects were not everywhere the same, but everywhere the situation was one of an "advanced" culture meeting a somewhat "primitive" one. The two culture worlds were moving in different directions and at different speeds. At their meeting, the frontier hunter and subsistence farmer generally found himself at a disadvantage whether he realized that fact immediately or not.

The first major brush with the outside during the Civil War illustrates features that have characterized most of the contacts since, although the violence of the war naturally exaggerates the essential elements of the contact situation. The events of the war had been shaped outside the region, and Little Smoky Ridge and its counterparts had no part in determining their form. Indeed, the neighborhood did not exist as a social entity until after the war, though the people who were to settle it were already moving in the direction of the Ridge. The war came to them from another world, but it influenced the course of their lives in a number of ways, as "Uncle" Eli can recall:

The War had a right smart effect around here. I've heard my mother talk about it. The Confederates came in past Grandpa Weber's. The road was full of them— the fields, too. They took everything they came across. There wasn't hardly any menfolk around, and the women had to hide all they could so the Rebels wouldn't get all their food. Things picked up some when the men got back from fighting, but war brings people down to destruction.

The Civil War affected the inhabitants of Boone and adjacent counties in much the same way it affected the entire Southern mountain area. There were no major battles in the county, but for three years small bands of both Union and Confederate troops, partisan raiders, and loosely organized, undisciplined guerrillas crossed and recrossed the county. They engaged in raids and pitched battles, skirmishing and foraging and destroying crops.

Like many other mountain counties, Boone County became known as a "hotbed" of Unionism. The whole Southern Appalachian region formed something of a cultural island in the midst of an otherwise nearly united South. The politically dominant plantation system of the Deep South was totally foreign to this area of self-sufficing small farms. There was little communication and still less sympathy between the two sections, and seventy per cent of the votes against secession in Tennessee's election of 1861 came from the eastern mountain counties.[2]

Most of the families now living in Little Smoky Ridge had members who joined the Yankees because "it was their principle," and Civil War stories are almost as current in the mountains today as they are in the Confederate strongholds of the South. One might speculate that tradition-directed cultures in which the past is also the present keep old events alive because they are recounted to each new generation as if they happened yesterday, not ninety years ago. In Little Smoky Ridge the ancient struggle is sometimes referred to as "the War between the Democrats and Republicans," and it is still important politically. There are no Democrats in the neighborhood today, although most deserted the Republican party temporarily to vote for Roosevelt at the height of the Depression years.

Altogether, East Tennessee furnished perhaps 15,000 men to the Union army. In addition, many stayed in the mountains as "Home Guards," using their skill with the rifle on conscript officers and other Confederates. Others hid from both sides, often joining lawless bands of marauders who preyed on the countryside. Since many Southern sympathizers knew the mountain country as thoroughly as the Unionists, life became a desperate game of hide and seek during the Confederate occupation from 1861 to 1863. Nor did the situation change

materially when Federal forces gained control of East
Tennessee in 1863.

The men returning to the branches of Big Smoky
Creek after the war found that what crops and animals
the women had been able to raise had gone mainly to
foraging troops. Poor but self-sufficient before, many
families were now destitute and had to start again from
nothing. Some seem to have become completely discouraged, for "Uncle" Eli remembers that his father
"never was much account after the War."

The Civil War and its aftermath of depression were
the first outside influences to seriously disturb the local
population. For many parts of the mountain region
this marked the beginning of almost continuous, though
not necessarily large-scale, contact. For other parts, isolation continued or contact was indirect until after
1900. Little Smoky Ridge settled back into its old ways
for a time after the war, but it was never again completely outside the influence of the national economy.

For most neighborhoods, there seem to have been no
sudden, sweeping changes; but trends which were to
become accelerated in the twentieth century had plainly
begun. Thus, a traveler in western North Carolina in
the 1880s could describe newly opened mica mines with
booming company-owned shanty towns, but in the same
county note:

All the way along the habitations were small log cabins, with one room, chinked with mud, and these were

far between; and only occasionally thereby a similar log structure, unchinked, laid up like a cob house, that served for a stable. Not much cultivation, except now and then a little patch of poor corn on a steep hillside, occasionally a few apple-trees, and a peach-tree without fruit. Here and there was a house that had been half-finished and then abandoned, or a shanty in which a couple of young married people were just beginning. Generally the cabins (confirming the accuracy of the census of 1880) swarmed with children, and nearly all the women were thin and sickly.

In the day's ride we did not see a wheeled vehicle, and only now and then a horse. We met on the road small sleds, drawn by a steer, sometimes by a cow, on which a bag of grist was being hauled to the mill, and boys mounted on steers gave us good evening with as much pride as if they were bestriding fiery horses.[3]

Even forty years later much the same could be said about the Tennessee side of the mountains near Little Smoky Ridge:

The high mountain fastnesses are uninhabited, but in the foothills or lower mountains, covered for the most part with second growth timber, live an interesting mountain folk. Here and there in the narrow valleys, log or perhaps frame houses are situated between steep hills with ribbon-like strips of grain or garden nearby. Patches of corn are cultivated on neighboring slopes with gradients of 25 or 35 degrees.[4]

Change seemed inevitable, however:

This condition will not exist much longer. The region is now being visited by an increasing number of tourists.

The Dixie and Lee highways enter the Valley from the north and connect with several excellent highways penetrating some of the most scenic parts of the mountains.[5] Change in this instance culminated in the establishment of the Great Smoky Mountains National Park, one of the largest resort areas in the East. In the resulting tourist boom of Cloudland, Tennessee, the natives have for once turned the exploitation tables on the "foreigners."

In Little Smoky Ridge the oldest residents cite the Civil War and its consequences as the first dramatic episode in the relations with the rest of the country. In the next breath, they are likely to mention the next important episode by saying, "Things didn't really pick up around here until the public works started in on Lusty and over on Big Creek." It was "public works," as any operations hiring large crews of workmen are called, that again "gave a man a chance to support his family." Beginning in the 1880s, for Little Smoky Ridge public works meant large lumber companies on the river in the next county and on numerous creeks in western North Carolina plus many smaller outfits.

To people in the mountains the public works seemed to appear suddenly. Actually they were part of a widespread awakening of American and foreign capital to the tremendous industrial potentialities of the South. They were the beginning of the New South which was then emerging, still shaky and uncertain, full of speculative dreams of economic development. Much of the capital came from outside the South, but the South responded enthusiastically.

The coal, iron, timber and water power resources of the Southern Appalachian and Piedmont regions readily attracted outside capital. In tapping these resources the larger companies introduced certain organizational schemes that were to have far-reaching consequences for the mountain inhabitants who came in contact with them. The most characteristic of these, the mining town and the lumber camp, are basically different social structures and therefore affected local society in somewhat different ways. On the whole, the mining town and similar company towns were more disruptive to the area socially and culturally than the lumber camp.

Even though deforestation with ridiculously low monetary compensation ultimately left the region and its citizens more impoverished than ever, the immediate effects of lumbering were not especially destructive. In many respects the operations suited already established work habits. Nor were wasteful methods likely to disturb a people who traditionally viewed the forests as a barrier to be destroyed whenever the need for crop land demanded.

If the frontiersman's first skill was hunting, his second was handling an ax. Every man was his own carpenter for most purposes, and the forests supplied wood for building, for household furnishing including most do-

mestic utensils, and for fuel. There were also many
local craftsmen who made wagons, doors, boxes, spokes,
cooperage and other wood products. Small scale lumbering was one of the earliest means for supplementing
income. Men brought down a few logs after the fall
harvest and floated them down river on the spring
"tides." There were always one or two families in Little
Smoky Ridge engaging in this practice.

Sawmills were also common in mountain neighborhoods long before the Civil War. They served local needs
adequately enough, turning out rough lumber for persons who supplied the logs from their own woodlands.
The Morgans in Little Smoky Ridge were associated with
such a sawmill for several generations, and the Jones
family today operates a similar small mill for local custom.

Large scale commercial exploitation of the Southern
Appalachian forests did not begin until an increasing
national market for timber combined with the railroad
building era to attract the necessary capital to the region.
Once begun, however, the lumber syndicates slashed their
way across the landscape, following the old routes of
penetration up the larger river valleys, then up the creeks
and branches to the tops of the mountains. They covered in twenty years the paths it had taken the pioneers
a century to follow, and they cleared more land in one
generation than the permanent settlers had cleared in
five or six. At first, selective cutting somewhat modi-

fied the course the lumber companies took; the finer cabinet woods went first. But finally, with the extension of rail transportation, the cheaper grades and smaller logs for the pulpwood and tannin extract industries all came under the ax.[6]

The depletion of the forests is revealed by the rapidly changing cutting standards as culling became the rule rather than the exception. In 1885, few logs under thirty inches in diameter were cut. Ten years later the usual cutting was 24 inches. By 1900, the average limit had dropped to 21 inches. By 1905, lumbermen were taking chestnut and oak only fifteen inches on the stump.[7] The boom was almost over by then. Lumber cutting in the region reached a peak in 1909. In that year there were more than 2,500 active sawmills in Tennessee. In the three counties affecting Little Smoky Ridge (Judson, Boone and Holston) there were over eighty sawmills operating in 1909, one of them cutting over 5,000,000 board feet annually.[8]

For natives of the area the big lumbering operations meant extra income in a period when making a living on mountain farms was becoming more difficult year by year. They gladly took cash for their land or for timber rights and also for wages, for most companies employed local labor. Some who sold their lands were allowed to remain as caretakers while others gravitated toward the larger sawmill sites that soon became towns. Still others began to leave the region to take employment in the new textile mills that were also part of the New South's industrial revolution.

As long as the lumbering boom lasted, a matter of only a few years in some places and as much as forty years in others, few within the mountains questioned the cutting methods of the big companies. Timber scouts, working in front of the advancing railroads, made their way into all parts of the Southern Appalachians purchasing thousands of acres for as little as one dollar an acre. Sometimes they were able to acquire the land through tax sales or by filing claims where titles were clouded. Only later did the original owners wake up to find themselves landless or on land now worthless and realize that they were again without a source of cash income.

For some of the worn out and overpopulated parts of the region the sale of timber lands worked little hardship. There were sections that were already being abandoned when the lumber companies first appeared on the scene. Brender and Merrick report this type of situation in parts of northern Georgia.[9] From the time of the first settlement between 1840 and 1850 population had increased there far beyond the ability of the land to support the frontier economy, and families were moving out all through the nineties. Land purchases by a lumber outfit at that time came as a welcome opportunity for the owners to realize some cash on land they were planning to leave anyway.

In other parts of the mountains, however, families remained on their land but took employment as lumberjacks, or sawmill operatives, or worked on the construction of logging roads and railroads. The big profits went to outside interests while local men gained only in wages or from the sale of timber rights. It was in this form that lumbering and the lumber camp began to touch Little Smoky Ridge in the 1880s. The first companies sawed only a limited amount of poplar. Then, in 1901, a company in neighboring Judson County began a broader enterprise that continued until 1938, although its greatest output came before World War I.

All the larger outfits maintained camps for their workers. "The camps were no place to take women and children." They never pretended to be more than temporary shelters for the several hundred men required to cut over any given tract. For that very reason the camps did little to alter traditional social organization in Little Smoky Ridge. A man who took forest employment did not give up his home and move his entire family. Instead, he left home by himself for a few weeks or months at a time in a manner quite familiar to frontier families whose menfolk were accustomed to long hunting and marketing trips. The rest of the family could continue to cultivate the land while the men worked in the camps. Eli Morgan expresses the general attitude thus:

I could get a dollar or a dollar and a half a day and buy flour and meat at the camp for my family. I'd been

working before for twenty-five to forty cents a day.
A man could plant out his corn just the same. I had
an awful good woman to work. She and the children
worked the corn while I was away. A man could work
the year round if he wanted. I came home weekends.
My woman expected me so I came, even one time when
I'd scalded my foot. The boss was pretty good to help
out or pay something if you had trouble in your family.
He helped when one of my girls was sick. I came home
then. I told the boss I'd be back when I got my family
straightened out, and he gave me an advance on my pay.

It is typical that Eli *told* the boss he would come back
to work after attending to family needs. He did not *ask*
permission to leave. Men from Little Smoky Ridge cannot conceive of themselves as subordinate to others in a
hierarchical system. Moreover, their first allegiance is
always to themselves or their families, not to the requirements of an industrial or other impersonal organization.
The lumbering companies seem to have been relatively
lenient and informal in their relations with the local population. So was the army during the Civil War. In more
recent years, however, some of the men have experienced
the rigidity of large industrial plants and of the modern
armed forces where their attitudes clash violently with
those of the authorities in these highly bureaucratic organizations.

For thirty to forty years the various kinds of work associated with lumbering provided the most dependable
non-farm source of income for the neighborhood—more

dependable than whiskey-making before Prohibition. But the bigger outfits were leaving the region by 1920, although many smaller operations have continued to come and go along the many creeks, culling old stands. They use small portable circular saws that can be set up or taken down in a few hours. The early ones used steam, but old truck or car engines drive the newer ones. Piles of sawdust at the foot of all the branches of Little Smoky Ridge and at several points along Big Smoky Creek attest the recent presence of small sawmills, but only one operates regularly in the neighborhood itself today. It belongs to Orville Jones, who values his equipment at about four hundred dollars. At least four related families derive some income from the mill which saws small amounts of timber from all the local ridges and from a few stands farther afield.

Owners fell their own trees and snake the logs down the mountain by mule team to be loaded onto trucks at several dumps in the neighborhood. Few persons cut more than half a dozen trees in a year, primarily for their own building and repairing needs. Small lots of low-grade lumber are also sold up and down the valley, and a few families sell "cording rights" to outsiders who cut firewood on Little Smoky Ridge for sale in town.

Whether families sell any wood products or not, their woodland acres represent a real asset, poor as the forests now are. Small second growth trees that have no market value are nevertheless adequate for local building needs

since houses and barns need not be elaborate to conform
to neighborhood standards. Family woodlots also supply
all necessary fuel since wood ranges and fireplaces are
used for cooking and heating. "Busting" logs and piling
the "chunks" are important masculine activities, especially in the fall. The final splitting into stove lengths
is generally considered a feminine job.

Just as in other economic matters there is no long range
planning for the use of wooded acres. A man cuts trees
when he needs the lumber himself or when he needs the
extra cash the trees may bring. There is no more attempt
to understand a fluctuating market in wood products
than in tobacco or beans. Scientific forestry is unknown. Nature gives and the farmer cuts. When nature
ceases to give, this is accepted fatalistically. Govern-
mental and other agencies have tried in recent years to
introduce better handling of woodlots in the region, but
none of the attempts has yet touched Little Smoky
Ridge.

Lumbering as a major economic activity has had its
day in the Southern Appalachian region. It came and
went, providing enough jobs to keep families on their
otherwise unproductive lands for another generation or
so. Because of the special nature of lumber camps and
the way they could be fitted into already present work
patterns, they produced no basic change in local social
organization. They did, of course, strip the region of a
major resource which has not been replaced. This fact

is recognized and regretted by the local population but without condemnation of the shortsighted methods that led to the present state. The regret is that there are no more opportunities for making money close to home.

The relatively minor modifications in traditional social organization required of those who participated in the region's lumber boom can be better appreciated in contrast to the major modifications produced by mining operations in other parts of the Southern Appalachians. The native population in the Allegheny-Cumberland Plateau province had much the same culture in the 1870s and 1880s when the coal fields there were first being exploited as did the people in the Blue Ridge-Smoky Mountain province. But the organizational form introduced by mine owners required major and permanent rearrangements in social organization that led eventually to the destitute mining communities that so shocked the nation in the 1930s.

Under the mining system of company-owned shanty towns, the frontier family exchanged its often precarious self-sufficiency for complete dependence on wages. Moreover, those who participated in the mining boom gave up much of their personal independence by moving into company housing. While they could not know it at the time, the move placed them in a position from which retreat would be, if anything, more difficult than from their small and deteriorating family farms.

Mining began to be important in parts of West Virginia, Kentucky, Tennessee, and Alabama at about the same time that lumbering was proceeding rapidly in these and other Southern Appalachian sections in the last quarter of the nineteenth century and first decades of the twentieth. The great industrial expansion of the period provided the capital, railroads for transportation, and a ready market for coal. There was also a potential labor force in the mountain farmers who were willing to relinquish lands and mineral rights and go to work for what seemed ample monetary compensation. The ever more pressing need for a cash income was an important factor in inducing many families to try the new occupation. There was probably no realization at first that return to their old ways would be practically impossible if the change proved unhappy.

Since all but a few mines required workers and their families to live on company property, becoming a miner meant giving up one's own property. Where a lumber worker could continue to plant crops, which his wife and family tended, the miner moved his entire family into a company house in a company town. Mining was thus a much more radical change and meant more than simply learning a new trade. It imposed a new way of life on the whole family, a way that involved adjusting to close neighbors who were also learning the new way. It also demanded reliance on a company store, company doctor, and the other company services for which deductions were made from the miner's pay, which as often as not was in company "scrip."

Company towns varied, of course, according to their size, the despotic or benevolent nature of managers, the ratio of native to outside labor, the general prosperity of the mining industry, and other factors. They were all alike, however, in transforming the old hunter-farmer who had been his own boss into a wage earner whose economic position forced him to obey the orders he often resented. As studies in the mining sections of the region reveal,[10] this kind of contact situation, far more than the lumbering situation, altered the core of traditional social structure. It placed families in a subordinate position to impersonal corporations. Families no longer had personal control over their activities, for to a large extent the company controlled not only the town but the families and persons of the miners through its economic power over them.

The completely dependent position of the Southern Appalachian coal miner became apparent to the country at large only during the Depression, but the coal industry had been failing ever since the final boom year of 1920. Companies had been abandoning mines and miners steadily since that time. As a result, the national depression more nearly prostrated the region's miners than those who had clung to their farms, sending their men occasionally to such wage work as was available.

But no group could completely escape the economic distress of the thirties.

By 1930, even the most remote mountain neighborhoods had been drawn sufficiently into the national economy to feel its ups and downs. In fact, their position on the fringes of the economy at the bare subsistence level of farming and at the lowest levels of cash income made them particularly vulnerable. Those who had ventured out into industrial areas as unskilled or semi-skilled labor found themselves without jobs or resources. Many returned to the mountains which represented home and the security of family, if not economic security. Their welcome at home was assured, but their presence added greatly to the already strained relief resources of mountain counties.

In Little Smoky Ridge "things were really bad back in the thirties." Products raised for home consumption did not decrease particularly during these years, but local acreages and soil conditions by that time were insufficient to meet the food needs of a family. All required more meat, meal, salt, soda and tobacco (the minimum essentials of Ridge life) than they could produce. Money was essential for additional food and for clothing which was no longer made at home. Ready cash had always been scarce, but for several years there were virtually no opportunities to earn money.

A number of relief programs financed and directed by outsiders from government agencies and also from the Mission tried to alleviate immediate distress. Occasionally public and private organizations worked together. At other times their programs tended to overlap.

The administration of WPA funds for road projects was frankly political. The local administrator simply called a meeting at one of the country stores and enrolled everyone who promised to "vote right" in the next election. Families from the Ridge could have qualified in legal fashion, but the method of presenting the funds got a heavy Democratic vote in a traditionally Republican district, thereby angering several workers at the Mission who were staunch Republicans. On the other hand, the Mission gladly accepted government funds to help run its relief center in Little Smoky Ridge.

The relief programs were only "stop gap" measures. They could not reverse long developing trends in the histories of neigborhoods like Little Smoky Ridge. The frontier culture was doomed, for the limitless lands necessary for its success were gone. The cultural demands of the rest of the country had brought exploitation of the region in a series of invasions beginning with the Civil War. Pressure from the outside is a continuing fact today in forms that will eventually substitute the ways of the outside world for the older culture. In this process the neighborhood will undoubtedly die as a separate social entity, for its economic resources are too limited to support a population at the standard of living demanded by modern American civilization.

CHAPTER SIX

The Family and its Cultural World

THE DAYS OF LITTLE SMOKY RIDGE ARE NUMBERED. AT the same time a certain core of old cultural forms and values remains to slow the process of change. These forms with their underlying social structure provide a basis for understanding the failure of the neighborhood to change readily to ways that would raise the material level of living. They also help to explain some of the friction and misunderstanding that occurs between the neighborhood and the outside world when the two meet.

Though frontier conditions of unlimited land and game no longer prevail, many of the values and attitudes of the frontiersman and his family remain. Most important of all, neighborhood life continues to center in the family, and family routine follows the time pattern of the early hunting and patch farming culture. In this routine, with its implied concept of time, the local way of life is at variance with modern American culture as a whole.

To a person accustomed to the clock-regulated, contractual relationships of American urban and industrial society, life in Little Smoky Ridge seems timeless and aimless. To a person in Little Smoky, however, time is ecological and structural, as those terms have been used by Evans-Pritchard.[1] Time is ecological in being based on man's response to changes in nature. It is structural in being a conceptualization of activities within a social group, primarily within the family. Time, thus, is not the *thing* that it is in most of American society. It is not something to be wasted or saved or cut into arbitrary units to which all events must then conform.

Calendrical dates and chronometric hours which are all important in the outer society are unimportant in the neighborhood. Instead, there is a rhythm of changing activities in response to the succession of seasons and the life history of individuals and families. In the rest of the country these structural and ecological rhythms tend to comply with the clocks and calendars used to measure them. In Little Smoky Ridge days and seasons slip by unmeasured or marked as special by births or deaths or unusual natural phenomena such as the "Big Snow" (1917) or "The Flood" (1938).[2] Even these soon blend into a nebulously defined past. Since the future is equally nebulous there is little planning in terms of days and years yet to come.

In the scattered households of the neighborhood, daily and seasonal routines vary considerably in specific detail but within a rather limited range of activities. Some of the simplicity of routine activity is explainable in terms of the extremely simple material basis of existence. Life is geared to self-sufficient survival with no special emphasis on the acquisition of material possessions as status symbols or even as labor saving devices.

The houses are all of simple log or frame construction with one to three small rooms and perhaps an additional loft or lean-to. They are from ten to seventy-five or eighty years old and were all built by family labor with sometimes the help of other neighbors. Although two men have recently cut logs for new houses, it may be years before they do the actual building.

The houses are old, but they are constantly in a state of remodeling which makes them ever different, ever adjustable to changing needs. In meeting the requirements of the changing family life cycle, they seem to be in a continual state of flux. Buildings once occupied by humans become barns or tobacco sheds and are later again used to shelter humans. There are almost infinite ways to alter a structure. An old door is boarded up, a new one cut. A loft is finished for storage and sleeping or torn out when the boards become more valuable for another purpose. A new room is added, first as an unchinked lean-to, later more solidly finished. Porches materialize on the front or back, and the space between floor and ground can be enclosed for additional storage room as needed.

All such alterations and repairs are leisurely. They may occupy a man continuously for a few days or be left for months in an unfinished state. There is some pressure to complete changes before cold weather. Still, if the work cannot be finished this year it surely can be done before another winter. Working in this spirit, Lum Bruton spent most of a summer tearing down a lean-to at the front of his mother's house and moving it, board by board, to the back. When the work made him "nervous" he stopped and went hunting. At one stage he left for North Carolina and was gone for several weeks. Finally, the stove was moved to the new lean-to, but final weather-proofing with cardboard cartons was not completed until long after cold weather began. Yet no one complained about this inconvenient, but perfectly natural, state of affairs.

In appearance and material conveniences all the houses fall far below general American levels, but all meet neighborhood standards which stress "good enough for Grandpa" rather than "keeping up with the Joneses." There is no running water or electricity, but these are not greatly desired. A few say, "It might be nice to have electric, but I'd be scared of it." Or they cite an example in a neighborhood woman who once had a gas motor washing machine that "tore up everything."

The greatest felt inconvenience of local housing is the distance to the spring or branch for water. Characteristically, the complaint is about the distance and not expressed as a desire for running water. Spring water is *known* to be superior for drinking to any water that comes through pipes. For heavy washing, most women keep their wash kettle by the branch rather than draw water to the house. As for the possibility of water-flushed toilets, the idea seems to strike most residents as somewhat frivolous.

The number of farm outbuildings varies but usually includes a tobacco barn, mule and cow shed, corn crib, hog pen, and often chicken coops. Like the houses, these are built by a man and his family in the same unhurried manner. For some months in 1949 Will McCoy talked about a new barn, and he and his sons began bringing down logs for it. Finally, one day when all the boys were home and several other men were visiting McCoy, all worked strenuously for several hours and raised the sides of the new structure to the height of three or four logs. The mule and cow were moved to their new quarters immediately, but it was months before the building had a roof.

There is little variation from one house to another in the kind and quantity of furnishings. Judged by, say, the illustrations in a Sears Roebuck catalog, all are poorly furnished. While people in Little Smoky Ridge frequently look at mail order catalogs, they do not judge themselves by what they see. They think more in terms of pride in the ability to "make do" with what they have.

In the past of course most articles were homemade. The men built bedsteads, tables, chairs, benches, chests and cupboards. They also made buckets, barrels, churns, trays, dishes, and baskets. And the women made all the clothing and bedding at home. Most of the pioneer arts have disappeared within the memory of the older generation to be replaced by the hit or miss remaking of secondhand goods and the useful resurrection of pieces discarded as worthless by others.

There is considerable ingenuity in patchwork construction on all furnishings. A formerly useless stove may acquire a pipe made from lard cans with the bottoms cut out. Or a keg is sawed in two and an old car seat placed across the halves to make a porch chair. An ancient school bus has furnished chairs for several families, and the bus body is now a corncrib in Elmer Morgan's yard.

The resulting assortments of odd beds, tables, chairs and other furniture crowded into small rooms give an appearance of confusion in all the homes. There are no cupboards or closets except for the inevitable "safes" for storing dishes or bedding, and most possessions hang from nails. It takes a stranger some time to realize that each nail and each suspended sack, purse, or suitcase has special contents belonging to a particular member of the family who can put his hands on any desired object in a moment.

Objects not readily suspended from nails are stored

in a variety of containers. The coffee tin of old nails and screws and the snuff jar with penknives and pencils stand on the mantel beside the lamp, the unused alarm clock, a few family photographs, perhaps some souvenirs of Holston or White City, and whatever small "pretties" the family possesses. Such treasured objects are on display if possible; otherwise they are carefully wrapped and stored away. Extra clothing and other bulky items are stored in cartons or flour sacks in the loft, under beds and tables, or under the house. The winter's supply of canned fruits and vegetables stands under beds and tables until needed.

Beds are the bulkiest items of furniture and cover most of the floor space except in the kitchen. Three persons to a bed is not unusual, but some families still need three or four beds. Because "staying the night" is common among friends and relatives, especially in times of sickness or death, there may be a dozen or more persons sleeping in a house at times. The kitchen is the only room without beds, and it has its own profusion of furnishings—the stove, table, meal bin, bench for buckets and wash basins, shelves for dishes, and an array of skillets and "stewcups" hanging over the stove. Chairs, which are always at a premium, are moved from kitchen to porch or other rooms as needed.

In matters of clothing also, the standards of Little Smoky Ridge are considerably simpler than in much of the rest of the country. All of the women sew, but factory goods have entirely replaced homespun materials. Some clothes are bought new, but many are handed down within the family or purchased second-hand to begin with, and there is the same ingenuity in remaking and patching clothing as there is in fixing furniture.

The men usually wear overalls and cotton shirts, although some of the younger men now occasionally wear cotton or wool slacks and gaudy shirts. Hats are worn both indoors and out, and overcoats are added in cold or wet weather. The women all wear cotton dresses the year round, adding a sweater or coat in chilly weather. Both men and women go barefoot a good part of the year.

Local living conditions often elicit shock and pity from Mission personnel and others who fail to comprehend the nature of neighborhood living and working standards in relation to family needs and a time pattern so different from their own. Neighborhood life flows along in terms of changing family situations and changing seasons. Work is accomplished in a setting of lifelong ties to kin and land, not by a rigid schedule of tasks that must be done at a certain time.

Since many of the pioneer activities have disappeared and the general level of living is lower than several generations ago, the present daily and seasonal round differs in detail from that of the past. But it is still more ecological and structural than clockbound. Families are more oriented to changing farming and hunting seasons than

to a forty-hour week. They are more often motivated
by immediate felt needs than by a compulsion to work
eight hours a day because work in itself has value or in
order to acquire material goods beyond minimum essentials. "Minimum essentials" may include an expensive guitar, but this does not commit a man to working
steadily after he has acquired the guitar.

The men do work away from home at times when
the need for money becomes urgent. They are more apt
to try to meet the need at home by distilling whiskey, a
course that does not seriously upset their routine or
threaten their position of dominance in the culture. In
a town job the man loses his freedom of movement and
trades his position of command in a patriarchal family
for a subordinate role in a wage labor system. Ordinarily
he cannot even bolster his ego by continued control of
his family, for they rarely accompany him on job hunting trips. If he stays home, on the other hand, his position is assured. He must provide for his family, but on
days he feels "too poorly" to work no one is likely to
press him. There is some neighborhood clicking of
tongues over two men who drink all day every day, but
on the whole it is considered in the nature of things for
men to do as they please.

At home the daily routine of men and women differs
considerably. In fact, the separateness of male and female spheres of activity is a striking feature of neighborhood life. The work of the men tends to be sporadic,

but this does not necessarily mean that they do less work than the women or than men in other regions. There is a popular stereotype of the shiftless mountaineer who spends his days lying against the side of the house nursing a jug of corn whiskey. The stereotype has a parallel in what some anthropologists term the "coconut tree theory" that primitive peoples are invariably lazy and disinclined to exert themselves to make a living. Such notions arise easily from a comparison of machine with non-machine economies, but they are not supported by fact.

The real disparity seems to lie in the differing imperatives of the two systems. An industrial economy demands regular hours of work, and these hours are the same for a majority of the workers. An agrarian economy gives the individual worker considerably more leeway and does not require close synchronization with other workers. The person in a non-machine society is relatively free to choose his own time for work or rest, and this is precisely what the men in Little Smoky Ridge do.

There are periods of great activity when a man plows, plants, harvests, or perhaps does some building. He may then leave home to wander if he pleases, for the men are familiar with all the mountain trails and think nothing of walking forty or fifty miles to visit friends. At home again work is done in spurts, and there are long hours to sit on the porch, relax at the store, or talk and drink with other men. In the course of a year, however, a man does spend a good deal of time and energy in work. It is the inefficiency of tools and techniques as much or more than any tendency to loaf that accounts for the relative unproductiveness of local labor.[3]

The women's routine is steadier and keeps them closer to home, from custom and desire as much as necessity. The women express great fear of travel beyond familiar landmarks, and they rarely venture farther from home than the stores and churches of the vicinity. This attitude on the part of the women is a definite factor in making a permanent move outside the area unlikely for most families. Town manners seem bewildering and even wicked to the women and in several instances where whole families have moved to town, it has been the wife's extreme homesickness that has brought them back to the Little Smoky Ridge.

Since all the housework, preparation of meals, and care of the children devolve on women, their work is more repetitive from day to day than that of the men, but the general attitude is similar. Speed and efficiency are not deemed especially virtuous, and there is no compulsion to finish a task at a particular time. Washing not done one day can be done the next. There is always time to sit and visit or to play with the children. The women are inclined to complain of their hard lot as compared with the men's, but they obviously have a good many hours in which to do their complaining. On the other hand, like the men, they do work long hours at times; but they take their ease pretty much when they please.

All households have a pattern of daily and weekly tasks which varies somewhat with the season and the number of daylight hours and with the size and age distribution of the family. Families are up before dawn, and some women cook beans, potatoes, and cornbread for the whole day in the early morning. Other women start a fire for each meal. Meal times depend on the day's activities as much as any regular time schedule. "Let's get us some dinner" may be said any time from 11:00 A.M. to 2:00 P.M. Members of the family usually eat together, but often the women serve the men and children first and sit down to their own food later. Visitors are invited to join the family with the simple phrase, "Come wash up if you want," which they do if they wish or which they refuse with an excuse, "No, I've done dinnered already."

Like the men, the women have fewer domestic duties than their grandparents. Spinning and weaving which formerly took much of a woman's time are unknown skills to the present generation. Quilting is the only major home art still practiced, and every house has a quilting frame either suspended from the ceiling or stored in the loft when not in use. Piecing and quilting are done especially in the fall when cold weather prevents outside work and also points the need to prepare for winter.

Although the number and kinds of tasks have changed through the years, an important fact of neighborhood life is that practically all activity—economic, educational, affectional, recreational—still transpires within the family circle which is the guiding structural unit of this society. The family is the center of the individual's universe. To a remarkable degree, it *is* his universe. Other systems such as school, government, church, or job are incidental, tangential, and only fleetingly important. On the other hand, a family that includes parents, siblings, grandparents, aunts and uncles, cousins, nieces and nephews, children and grandchildren, is always there. The view of himself and the world which the individual learns in this setting is not easily unlearned when he finds himself in other settings.

It is only a slight exaggeration to say that Little Smoky Ridge would not be a recognizable neighborhood grouping without its kinship linkages between households. Geographic propinquity strengthens the relationships, but alone it cannot account for the ties between households. At the same time, kinship and geography help to maintain lines of antagonism which are also important to the neighborhood's existence, for family pride and unity in this culture seem to make for some degree of hostility toward all other families.

Little Smoky Ridge is thus a system of both positive and negative social relations in a particular geographic and cultural setting. The accompanying diagram and chart of major kinship lines show the two major and two minor family groups of the neighborhood. When all possible blood and marriage lines are considered, it is evident that every household is linked in some degree with every other household. Actually, distinctions are made between persons who are "a whole lot of kin" and those just "a little bit of kin," and some links are forgotten entirely. In practice there is strong antagonism between Group I and Group II, and Groups III and IV tend to identify with Group I. It should be mentioned that Group II has strong ties to another neighborhood just west of Little Smoky. The groups are not completely rigid, however, and some households are only loosely allied with their family group. Relationships also change through time; for example, a recent marriage between Houses 16 and 17 has created a slight link between parts of Groups I and II.

It is conventional to think of a neighborhood as a unit of co-operating families living in a small area. Yet it seems important to note that sustained hate as well as sustained love requires the constant presence of the person toward whom the emotion is directed. The antipathy between Group I and Group II is long standing, and the hostilities provide a form of recreation and emotional outlet for the members of both groups as well as serving

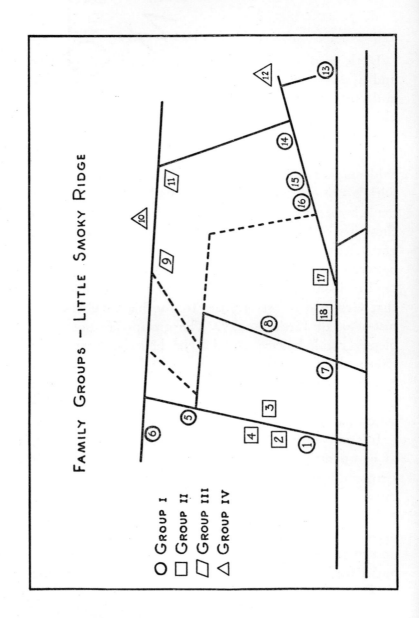

FAMILY GROUPS – LITTLE SMOKY RIDGE

O GROUP I
□ GROUP II
▱ GROUP III
△ GROUP IV

MAJOR KINSHIP LINES IN LITTLE SMOKY RIDGE

(Numbers refer to numbered houses on diagram.)

GROUP I   (Morgans and Browns)

1. *Print and Sula McCoy.* Sula is sister to Lily Morgan (5) and Lon Brown (6). Print is half-brother to Will McCoy (16).

5. *Eph and Lily Morgan, Eli Morgan.* Eli is half-brother to Dan Johnson (12), uncle to Robert Johnson (10), father to Mat Morgan (13), Jim Morgan (14), and Dora Morgan (15), also uncle to Elmer Morgan (15) and Jennie McCoy (16). Eph is son to Elmer and Dora Morgan (15), nephew to Jennie McCoy (16), brother to Pearl Weber (8). Lily is sister to Sula McCoy (1) and Lon Brown (6).

6. *Lon Brown.* Brother to Sula McCoy (1) and Lily Morgan (5).

7. *Clyde and Sarah Stinnot.* Sarah is sister to Jay Weber (8).

8. *Jay and Pearl Weber.* Jay is brother to Sarah Stinnot (7), Pearl is granddaughter to Eli Morgan (5), daughter of Elmer and Dora Morgan (15), niece to Jennie McCoy (16), Mat Morgan (13), and Jim Morgan (14), sister to Eph Morgan (5).

13. *Mat and Ruth Morgan.* Mat is son to Eli Morgan (5), brother to Jim Morgan (14) and Dora Morgan (15), uncle to Eph Morgan (5), and Pearl Weber (8). Ruth is sister to Lena Jones (11).

14. *Jim and Molly Morgan.* Jim is son to Eli Morgan (5), brother to Mat Morgan (13) and Dora Morgan (15), uncle to Eph Morgan (5) and Pearl Weber (8).

15. *Elmer and Dora Morgan* (a first cousin marriage). Elmer is nephew to Eli Morgan (5) while Dora is Eli's daughter. Elmer is sister to Jennie McCoy (16). Dora is sister to Mat Morgan (13) and Jim Morgan (14). They are parents of Eph Morgan (5) and Pearl Weber (8).

16. *Will and Jennie McCoy.* Will is half-brother to Print McCoy (1). Jennie is niece to Eli Morgan (5), sister to Elmer Morgan (15), aunt to Eph Morgan (5) and Pearl Weber (8).

GROUP II   (Floyds and Brutons)

2. *John and Martha Bruton.* John is son to Eliza Bruton (4), brother to San and Lum Bruton (4) and Mina Randolph (17), nephew to Lige Floyd (3).

3. *Lige and Cora Floyd.* Lige is half-brother to Eliza Bruton (4), uncle to San and Lum Bruton (4) and to John Bruton (2) and Mina Randolph (17).

4. *Eliza Bruton, sons San and Lum Bruton.* Eliza is mother to John Bruton (2) and Mina Randolph (17), half-sister to Lige Floyd (3).

to strengthen intrafamily loyalties by means of frequent comparisons.

This feuding seems to be another part of the frontier culture, an expression of the frontiersman's deep conviction that he must let no slight pass and must never let another get the best of him. Troubles arise from a variety of overt causes, but the particular incident is less important than the traditional reaction. Individuals are quick to impute evil and wickedness to others while always picturing themselves as gentle and just. The incidents occasionally produce violence, but the more common procedure is to threaten lawsuits. The "law" which in some other contexts is resented is, in such instances, interpreted as a legitimate personal weapon for equalizing insults and injuries. The readiness to see antagonism as a component of any relationship is no doubt

---

17. *Wes and Mina Randolph.* Mina is daughter to Eliza Bruton (4), sister to San and Lum Bruton (4) and John Bruton (2), niece to Lige Floyd (3).

18. *John and Jean Mason.* A first cousin of John in a nearby neighborhood married a daughter of John Bruton (2). John may also be a nephew to Eliza Bruton (4).

GROUP III (Jones)

9. *Jim and Maggie Jones, son B. J. and family.* Jim and Maggie are parents to Orville Jones (11).

11. *Orville and Lena Jones.* Orville is son to Jim and Maggie Jones (9), brother to B. J. (9).

GROUP IV (Johnson)

10. *Robert and Elva Johnson.* Robert is son to Dan Johnson (12), nephew to Eli Morgan (5).

12. *Dan Johnson.* Dan is half-brother to Eli Morgan (5), father to Robert Johnson (10), uncle to Mat Morgan (13), Jim Morgan (14) and Dora Morgan (15).

another factor in making adjustment to outside employment difficult.

Geographic nearness *without* kinship defines the lines
of antagonism, but the lines are not invariable. Sometimes the women of two families remain on speaking
terms while their men are "lawing," although women
contribute their share to keeping feuds alive. Even when
strife between families is hottest, there is effective communication among all households and the flow of gossip
and news throughout the neighborhood is not inter-
rupted. And the cultural cohesiveness of the neighborhood becomes apparent in the reaction to outsiders.
When a stranger enters the foot of any branch, his presence and usually his business is quickly relayed, especially
by the children, to everyone. Whether welfare agent or
truant officer or something else, all are ready when he
calls.

Geographic nearness *with* kinship defines the lines of
most frequent interaction in the neighborhood, and these
are the lines that sustain the individual. Occupation of
a common territory is an important component of the
family system, for even close blood ties eventually break
down when family members have left the area.

In most respects kinship structure in Little Smoky
Ridge resembles that described by Parsons for the United
States as a whole.[4] In certain important particulars,
however, it varies in the direction of an older American
family form, that of the early frontier.[5]

In some places of course, the American frontier was settled by colonies of persons sharing some common religious or ethnic background. They built planned communities which from the start had legal, educational, religious and other facilities that transcended the family. But the more common form of settlement, the one found in Little Smoky Ridge, was that of the isolated family homestead. Some children in every generation moved on to new territories, but others married and settled on their parents' land or on nearby tracts. In this way, two or three original families have become so linked and branched through several generations of intermarriage that the neighborhood is truly kinship-based in its structure.

The family in Little Smoky Ridge has a patriarchal bias no longer found in most of the rest of the country. The husband and father is clearly master of the household and the ultimate decision maker. He takes orders from none (except perhaps older male relatives) while his wife and children need his permission for many of their actions. In some households he is genuinely feared. In others much is made verbally of his strictness, but the rest of the family seem to use his alleged fierceness as an excuse for refusing invitations they do not want to accept.

Nevertheless the family is not patriarchal in any sense of giving preference to paternal over maternal lines in reckoning descent. Local marriages do not show any strong tendency to extend lineages on the patrilineal side. There are at present six couples in which both husband and wife grew up in Little Smoky Ridge, five couples in which the woman came into the neighborhood at marriage, and five couples in which it was the man who came into the neighborhood at marriage. There are nine bachelors and only one unmarried girl over eighteen, but unless most of the men bring wives into their parents' homes, there would seem to be as much tendency toward matrilineal as toward patrilineal extension. Where both partners are local, relations remain close with both families. The situation is much the same as that reported by Brown for eastern Kentucky.[6]

An important feature of the kinship structure is the sense of closeness not only between a couple's family of procreation and their families of orientation but also between these and all collateral lines. In other words, Parson's "inner circle" combines with his "outer circle" to form one large kinship group. Again, this is reminiscent of the early American family.

In a kinship-based neighborhood of this sort the individual interacts almost exclusively with relatives, both paternal and maternal and of several generations. Children spend the first six to eight years of their life in nearly continuous contact with members of their family. Even later, contacts with non-relatives may be extremely limited. The situation is ideal for absorbing traditional behavior. The ways and values acquired in this manner happen not to be suited to an industrial civilization, but they make for security and self-assurance so long as the individual remains in the traditional setting.[7] He develops a strong sense of unity with his family but finds little or no opportunity to learn to co-operate with persons outside the family, and much of what he learns tells him *not* to co-operate with others.

In the midst of many relatives the individual grows into the family and its special cultural world with a minimum of conscious training. Beyond recognizing a helpless period of infancy and babyhood, neighborhood life draws few distinctions between children and adults. There is a clearcut division between masculine and feminine behavior, but not between adult and child behavior. Most activities include males of all ages or females of all ages. There is no "talking down" to the young who rapidly learn to imitate their elders in work and leisure activities.

As might be expected in a society not recognizing an extended childhood and adolescence, there is a relatively long babyhood. This is a period of great attention and indulgence with a minimum of responsibilities. It is also a period in which the sex roles which later become so important are almost completely ignored. Both boys and girls wear dresses until they are four or five, and the later favoritism toward males is not apparent. A baby of either sex is fondled, petted, played with and carried anywhere the mother goes. Babies are the center of attention at all gatherings and pass freely from one woman's arms to another's. The men, also, take an interest, but their interest seems to increase as the child begins to walk.

Babyhood continues for two or three years after a child learns to walk. There are few prohibitions or punishments, and children play alone or with siblings and cousins, with whatever they can find to amuse themselves. Coercion of small children is considered "mean," and the youngsters set their own schedules for rising, eating, sleeping, and the like. They are soon following the adult pattern. The frequently-heard threats of whipping seem to contradict the foregoing statements, but such threats are little more than a popular game enjoyed by all. More effective in keeping the children close to home are threats of "boogers," wildcats, and snakes uttered convincingly by mothers who themselves fear such creatures.

Actual whippings do occur. They are administered by the men and are likely to occur in fits of temper which have only indirect relation to the children's deeds. There seems to be an undercurrent of violence in the masculine culture which erupts in fights with other men and also at home, especially when the men have been drinking heavily. Such behavior is fully expected by the women and children. It is feared but not particularly condemned. However, there is a tendency in most homes for the women and small children to form a close circle that strengthens the concept of the male as an unpredictable creature to be feared.

From babyhood the individual moves quickly into what can best be described as miniature adulthood. For a boy the transition is symbolized by his first pair of overalls. He now begins to "make a man," which means he forsakes the world of women to follow his father and older brothers everywhere they go. He may still play with girls at times, but he leaves them immediately when there are men around who would tease him. And he no longer pays any attention to commands or suggestions from women, although the men control him readily enough when they wish.

There is little in their early experience to teach the boys much discipline or self-control; thus the stage is set for later difficulties if the man goes into the army or to employment that calls for discipline. Girls, on the other hand, learn to subordinate their desires to those of the men and to help with the housework and care of the younger children. They are constantly with their mothers in a feminine world since the men and boys are apt to be out of the house most of the day. A mother and daughters, even very young ones, talk and work in a "woman to woman" relationship just as the fathers assume a "man to man" role with the boys.

Both boys and girls participate in all adult gatherings. They call relatives of all ages by first name and are freely included in conversations. Since the most important neighborhood recreation is visiting, the children have ample opportunity to hear all the neighborhood and family business. They also learn to take part in the constant teasing and joking which mark all friendly and intimate relations in Little Smoky Ridge. The rather broad local humor has important functions beyond mere entertainment. It seems to be the principal form of social control in inducing children to assume adult roles, in uniting young and old, and in establishing workable relations between men and women. Indeed, joking seems to be the main bridge between the male world and the female worlds which are so far apart in many respects.

In growing up, neither sex receives any of the driving goals and ambitions to follow careers that so beset middle class American children in towns and cities. Their horizon is bounded by family and neighborhood. The future does not call for planning. By the time they reach school age they have already accepted continuation of the family with its cultural forms as a fact of existence. Early social maturity is thus a factor in the later rejection of ideas from other cultural systems.

All of the children now receive a few years of irregular schooling, begun later and ended earlier than in most regions. Going to school as they do after six to eight years of uninterrupted conditioning in the traditional family system, they are not motivated to study subjects which have no immediate meaning in the local scene. The compulsion to be a man or a woman as defined by

their own society is a strong one, and courting interferes
with school for the older boys and girls who, of course,
are already doing adult work at home.

In a sense, courting begins about the time a child
starts changing into a miniature adult. As soon as the
sex roles become differentiated, teasing about prospective
mates plays a big part in the child's life. "Who's your
woman?" or "Where's that man of yours?" are questions asked of any youngster. Names of children are
linked as each other's "man" and "woman," and the
whole neighborhood conspires to pester them about the
alleged relation. By adolescence the joking has serious
overtones and reflects preferences a boy or girl may have
confided to friends in secret but which soon become
public property.

Courting occurs openly between young people at all
social gatherings in homes and especially at church meetings. In fact, the whole trip to church is a courting
expedition for the teen-age group. The girls leave home
a few minutes before the boys, and the separate groups
gain recruits at each house along the trail. All at once
the boys begin a series of attacks, maneuvering to slap
their favorite girl on the back, pull her hair, or jostle
against her and then retreat before she can retaliate.
The girls pretend annoyance or indifference but make
no real effort to get away. The play continues at houses
near the church. The girls make a show of avoiding the
boys by entering the back door if the boys have gone to

the front porch. The girls soon appear at the front door, however, and are met with such comments as, "Hey, that man of yours just left; you better go chase him!" The girls reply in kind, and the horseplay continues until church time.

There are no formal announcements, but everyone knows when a marriage is in the offing. When a couple walk home together instead of in the separate sex groups there can be no doubt about the seriousness of the relation. They will also be seen holding hands wherever they go. Their actual wedding plans will be a secret until the day they slip away to the county seat with two friends for witnesses to have a justice of the peace marriage. On their return there will be a few days of neighborhood flurry over the event. After that, they settle into a vacant house confidently expecting to continue the family cycle which is the base of neighborhood existence. But they face the prospect of making a living with a cultural background no longer suited to actual conditions.

CHAPTER SEVEN

Supernatural Sanctions

TRADITIONAL CUSTOMS AND HABITS ASSOCIATED WITH
a strong family system continue to guide everyday behavior in Little Smoky Ridge. There are also strong religious sanctions for continuing traditional ways in the
fundamentally fatalistic approach of the neighborhood
to the supernatural. Many aspects of life that have long
since been taken over by science and a variety of secular
specialists in most of American society are interpreted
here as unalterable ways of God. Natural and supernatural are not neatly and permanently separated, and
natural phenomena are never entirely outside the realm
of supernatural explanation.

Even where knowledge of natural phenomena is em-
pirical, there is a feeling that much of nature is mysterious and beyond the power of man to predict or
control. It is God who controls human destiny and to
interfere with His ways would be foolhardy if not actually sacrilegious. In this sense the local religion is far
more absolute and much less critical than most modern
religion where man seems to control God. But in Little

Smoky Ridge good and bad, black and white are believed to be irrevocably set by God and revealed by Him in the Bible.

With all the unquestioning faith in ultimate supernatural sanctions, however, there is no accompanying sanction for formal church organization of the sort represented, say, by the nearby Mission at Russell Cove. Religion in Little Smoky Ridge does not require the constant practice implied by regular church attendance. Religion is something one either has or does not have as the result of a conversion experience. A person is either "saved" or "unsaved." There is no more middle ground in this than in other personal relations.

Neighborhood families are not interested in quiet Sunday after Sunday social preaching of the sort that characterizes many urban churches. A better life on earth is deemed less important than the assurance of future reward in heaven, and future reward depends on salvation granted by the grace of God through Jesus as a personal savior. Religious services must stir souls to repentance and to the achievement of a positive and intimate relation with God.

The local religion requires periodic reaffirmation in emotionally charged meetings, but it needs little in the way of formal church machinery. Its practices almost preclude weekly ceremonies around the calendar, for it is doubtful whether the high pitch of feeling that marks successful religious experience could be maintained in frequent, routine church attendance. As staunchly religious Maggie Jones avers, "If you don't have enough [religion] to last from one July to the next, you don't have it."

The yearly revival is the accepted means of maintaining supernatural standards, but alone it does not meet all religious needs. Every few years there are additional flurries of intense religious excitement that sweep through the area, purging whole neighborhoods of their sense of sin and restating basic values of man's defenselessness before the mighty power of God. They last a few weeks or months in a series of prayer meetings conducted by individuals who feel called by God to arouse sinners. By definition, all unsaved persons are sinners. Although most of the movements die quickly, some achieve a measure of stability around some particularly strong leader in which case they acquire a church building and may even extend their influence to other sections as recognized sects. They seem to be modern examples of the kind of religious "awakenings" that gave rise to so many now semi-secularized American denominations.

Such movements are possible because, in theory, any man is potentially a preacher who may gather a following and establish a church. He needs only conversion and a powerful compulsion to bring others to salvation, too. Frequently he himself has been a notorious sinner, drinking and "frolicking," as old "Uncle" Eli Morgan did before he was called in his youth to exhort others to accept Jesus and forsake their worldly ways. Understandably, there are doubts about the man when he suddenly changes his ways and begins to travel about the countryside holding prayer meetings. The saying is, "He's trying to make a preacher," and many watch him with suspicion. Some may eventually accept him, but as many others will reject his claims.

In this manner a variety of religious leaders with their fluctuating congregations have come and gone in Little Smoky Ridge. Viewed objectively, the differences between them are not great. All are Fundamentalist in the sense of accepting the Bible as the divinely revealed Word of God. Since supernatural sanctions outweigh human authority, secular knowledge must yield to Biblical passages. Faith in the infallibility of the Bible, however, does not prevent bringing the interpretation of particular preachers into question. Devoted followers have complete faith in the preacher of their choice while considering all others in error. Congregations splinter easily over matters of Biblical interpretation. The splits further follow customary lines of kinship or antagonism. The initial intensity of a religious awakening may temporarily unite several preachers and a number of ordinarily disagreeing families, but long standing habits reassert themselves, dispersing most movements before they achieve permanent organization.

A movement that stirred Little Smoky Ridge and adjacent neighborhoods in the fall of 1951 is representative. At its height it reached a feverish pitch of nightly prayer meetings in homes scattered over ten miles of mountainous countryside, wherever a family requested spiritual help. Three or four preachers and from thirty to fifty persons attended each meeting, but in a few weeks the fervor had died. Some of the participants joined a nearby Church of God, but most returned to their former ways of irregular attendance at revival meetings without permanent church affiliation.

A meeting held at Elmer Morgan's during the peak of the movement demonstrates the characteristic religious behavior of the neighborhood. I give the account here as recorded in my field log the following day. The notes seem to catch the pace and rhythm of the meeting better than more formal sentences would, and rhythm is the very heart of local religious performances.

Full moon showed two or three cars and a truck in the yard. Heavy clouds of smoke from the chimney indicated a roaring fire in the living room. A few men and boys were standing in the yard, a family was just getting out of one car. The living room was crowded with women and children around all sides. Men were standing in the doorways and visible in the two other rooms. Chests and tables supplemented the too few chairs, and the bus seat had been brought in from the porch.

The meeting was already in progress, and a quiet little man from another community was standing in the middle of the floor. He was not well known, and his cheap suit set him apart from the other men who were all in overalls. But he had their attention, eyes were wide, a few were already on the verge of tears.

The little preacher repeated his theme over and over. He was laying up treasures in heaven, which is the only place they have any value. He had been raised a Christian boy, but he had fallen into sin, going up and down the roads, going to shows, looking everywhere except in church for fun. But he hadn't been happy one minute of that whole time, until he found the Lord again and started laying up treasures.

There were "amens" and "that's sos" from men and women. Then he ended quietly, a little hesitant, not sure he had said anything to help them.

Then Brother Mercer, a preacher from down river, jumped into the theme of laying up treasures, loudly proclaimed that his first brother had said a great deal to help everyone. In seconds Brother Mercer fell into a rhythmic pattern of body movements and speech mannerisms. He bent his knees slightly, swaying first to one side, then to the other, then trembled erect and started again. He uttered a string of short sentences and phrases, punctuated with "aahs" to mark their rhythm. He spoke rapidly, several times a normal rate, until staccato phrases blended into each other and only ones he repeated over and over could be caught clearly.

He, too, had sinned and backslid many times. He found the Lord after turning away and refusing Him. He had promised to preach and not done it. But now he was on the right track and preaching because that was the only important thing to do. The Lord had called him and he had to keep going. He hadn't had more than two nights' sleep in the last four weeks, but he had to keep going. People asked him why he didn't rest, asked him how he could keep going so long, but he had to. The Lord gave him strength.

Brother Mercer doesn't have much down here on earth, nothing down here in the mirey clay, nothing to lose and heaven to gain. And he *is* going to heaven where he'll shake the nail-scarred hand of Christ and take his place on the right side of that golden throne and walk along the streets of heaven. He'll shake the hand of his father he loved more than anything on earth and of a brother recently struck dead by lightning.

Brother Mercer can't read a sweet word here on earth but he does what the Lord tells him no matter what anyone says. He'll shout and jump just as he's done in other meetings if the spirit moves him. (General laughter here as everyone knows his jumping antics and they agree with his sentiments.)

Mercer began to slow down, speaking normally again, mopping his perspiring brow, seeming ready to give over to another preacher until several men and girls began a hymn which reminded him of a few more things he wanted to say. He worked into the rhythm again, but somewhat slower.

Suddenly a woman's scream pierced the room, and a body whirled across the floor, twisting and stamping. She fell against others who were all on their feet now. They pushed her away and she bounded from arms to arms and suddenly skipped to a stunned stop against the wall, shaking her head as if not sure where she was.

At the same time a low mumble began in another corner, steady and droning. In a monotone with lips barely moving a woman debated with herself the choice between heaven or hell, one. No one paid any attention.

Then a third preacher, Dallas Mason, came forward. He is young, very nervous, eyes wild and bright. He jerked forward in the throes of a weighty problem that had him so worked up he could hardly speak. Waving his arms and frequently running his hand through his hair, he told of a dream he had last night. He wasn't sure he should speak about such terrible things, but he had to as the Lord had directed him. His theme was women who wear shorts; they might just as well go naked. They'd better tear off their clothes, go naked, if that was what they wanted.

He used the same bending of knees and swaying erect again, only with more trembling and shaking and wilder use of his arms than Brother Mercer. He seemed obsessed with women and sex and their sinfulness but finally changed his theme to the necessity of preaching. You've got to preach the whole Bible from lid to lid, every verse of it. There's a terrible day approaching. The mark of the beast is the only prophecy not yet fulfilled, and when that comes there'll be some people find themselves in hell.

The meeting was winding up with singing and general participation, some weeping, others shouting and happy, repeating "sweet name of Jesus." Several were spinning and reeling, shaking hands with each other, laughing, joyous. But others turned their attention to prayer for the mourners. Finally all were kneeling, swaying, praying aloud each in his own words but all voices assuming the same rhythm. Finally two penitents "came through for Jesus" and all rose, happy, gay, laughing, greeting fellow Christians as the group began to disperse.

The values affirmed by the group—treasures in

heaven, no need to "read a sweet word here on earth," nothing worthwhile "down here in the mirey clay," the sinfulness of worldly pleasures and emotions, the importance of ecstatic religious states, and the necessity for preaching the Bible "from lid to lid"—are common to many sects that have special appeal for the socially, economically, or emotionally impoverished of the world. They fit present conditions. They were also present and suited to conditions on the early frontier.

The whole frontier tradition continues to strengthen and reinforce revivalism and an informal, lay church organization in the Southern Appalachians. The settlers who flocked into the region after the Revolution did not come, for the most part, from the classes that were active members in the established churches of the old colonies. There were relatively few ministers among them and isolated neighborhoods of scattered homesteads could not support a church and ministry if they wanted to.

The older denominations with their insistence on formal training for the clergy made little headway on the frontier. The rapidly proliferating sects of Baptists, Methodists, and certain renegade Presbyterians were more adaptable. They recruited preachers directly from the people and did not worry about their educational qualifications. It was their efforts that led to the early religious awakenings that so stirred the Southern Appalachian area at the close of the eighteenth century. They planted the seeds of the camp meeting, the revival, and the Fundamentalist sect that have continued to be important in the region ever since.[1]

Out of the movements on the early frontier grew a highly informal church organization that still obtains through much of the region.[2] The arrangement represents an adjustment by sparsely settled, economically poor, and familistic neighborhoods to meet their need for religious expression and periodic "renewal" of faith. The center of this loosely organized system is the simple one-room church designed to be used exclusively for preaching.

Since most neighborhoods cannot support their own minister, one man serves as many as four neighborhood churches, preaching in each about once a month. In addition, most ministers supplement their income with another occupation, usually farming. At present Little Smoky Ridge lacks even this arrangement, but families who wish to attend church have several choices in the surrounding neighborhoods or they may attend the Mission Sunday school in their own.

Monthly preaching keeps a neighborhood church loosely running through the year, but it is the annual summer revival, or protracted meeting that recruits new members and returns backsliders to the fold. The themes and values of the revival meeting are the same ones seen in the prayer meetings, but their expression is more rigidly confined in a preaching framework. The preacher is more completely in control of the situation, though congregational participation may be great. The revival preacher also seems more consciously aware of the effect his actions have on the group.

There is likewise more conscious symbolization of the themes in the selection of special hymns. Songs throughout the service stress the insignificance of worldly goods compared with heavenly treasures. Favorites include: "This world is not my home. . . . My treasures are laid up somewhere beyond the blue"; "Will you meet me over yonder and with happy millions dwell?"; "Oh, they tell me of a home far beyond the skies." Songs toward the end of the service emphasize making the decision for salvation: "Oh, why not tonight? Wilt thou be saved, then why not tonight?"; "Almost persuaded"; "Are you washed in the blood, the soul-cleansing blood of the Lamb?"

The revival sermon is considered the epitome of good preaching and serves as a model for all preaching services. Preachers are judged good or bad to the degree they can emulate the anticipated revival style. The one essential requirement for a sermon is that it stir the souls of sinners in need of repentance and that it should frighten the devil to the very marrow of his bones if he is hovering about.

The preacher takes a Biblical text and develops it, not into a logical discourse, but into a cadence punctuated by Biblical phrases. Between the Biblical words he intersperses personal anecdotes of souls "weeping in sin" that he has helped save. As he progresses his whole body sways, he paces and gestures, his voice rises to a shout and then drops to a whisper. He warns the congregation that they *must* make a decision either for heaven or hell. He exhorts them, "Don't wait until it's too late." Or again, "I see backsliders here who are worse off than sinners. God will smite the sinners who shut Him out, and there are sinners here tonight who will be smitten before another revival comes their way."

Finally the call comes for repentant sinners. This is the time of greatest congregational participation. There have been occasional shouts, responses, prayers and weeping as well as designated periods of singing before, but now all who are saved join in persuading the unsaved. The Christians—that is, those already saved—move to the front of the church to sing the hymns of persuasion. From time to time individuals break from the group to give more personal help to those who still hesitate at the back of the church. They take a sinner by the hand, urging him to accept Christ, or they weep and pray silently over him. A few resist stubbornly, either unable or unwilling to make the necessary move. But by the end of the week of morning and evening meetings there will be many newly professed and renewed Christians.

Before the neighborhood resumes its normal activities after a revival there is usually a baptism service for the new Christians. The prayer meeting movement of 1951 also culminated in a mass baptizing at a pool often used

for that purpose in a creek some two or three miles from
Little Smoky Ridge. Total immersion is required, and
cold water seems to be especially efficacious. Some who
have heard of churches in town that use warm water in
the baptismal tank say contemptuously, "They can't
have much religion if they have to warm the water."

Baptizings, like other religious meetings, bring together families from a number of neighborhoods. The
crowd assembles in leisurely fashion over a period of
hours on the appointed day, visiting or waiting quietly
until the appearance of the preacher and robed candidates signals the beginning of the ceremony. Only then
does the sacred nature of the gathering become apparent
in hymn singing and long prayers on the creek bank. At
last the sheeted principals are led into the water, one by
one, to be immersed and blessed by the preacher who
stands waist deep in the pool throughout the service.
There is less overt emotionalism than at the preceding
revival, perhaps because the wrestling with sin has already been accomplished and baptism is merely a final
seal on conversion. Also, there is some concern on the
part of preacher and candidates at least to get through
and change into dry garments. Families begin leaving
immediately except for a few who remain for a session of
hymn singing in a church or house not far from the
baptizing pool.

Baptism may be said to mark the end of the season of
intensive ritual, but it does not mark any sharp change

from sacred to secular sanctions. Supernatural and natural are interwoven in all activities throughout the year.
"God's will," "The wrath of God," and similar phrases
are the final explanation for many phenomena from
crops and weather to sickness and death. Moreover, for
every area of secular knowledge and techniques there
are corresponding areas of supernatural knowledge and
magico-religious techniques. This is particularly true in
matters of basic survival such as the success of crops or
the maintenance of health in humans, but in most aspects
of the culture the line between the practical and the
mysterious is extremely hazy.[3]

Most important, family and religious values comple-
ment and reinforce each other at the very heart of the
society in times of stress. This is true in times of unusual
disaster such as the flood in 1938. It is equally true for
the more predictable life crises. Probably no other event
is more realistically and at the same time more non-
realistically treated than death. Certainly none shows
more clearly the mutual roles of family solidarity and
religion in smoothing the transition from crisis to calm.

Other events may be treated matter-of-factly. Some
ritual, but no real ceremony, surrounds birth. Marriage
is a trip to the justice of peace and a day or two of joking
attention afterward. But death is disturbing to all for
many days before and after its occurrence, for death
brings to the fore all the fatalism, all the fear and hope
of future reward, and all the ties with living and dead

relatives which are so important in Little Smoky Ridge.

As death approaches, relatives come from all the surrounding area. They bring food and coffee and settle down to all night watches, ministering to the sick person, recalling other last illnesses, singing and praying, and waiting for the end. After a death, all the details of the final days are remembered and repeated frequently, often with a supernatural twist. There are many stories of persons in apparently robust health who seemed to have a premonition of death. They suddenly began to visit all the relatives they had not seen for years. On returning home, they were soon stricken ill and died in a few days. Actions and words of the dying take on special significance. For example, relatives who had watched "Uncle" Eli's apparently unchanging condition for a week knew the end was near the day he raised himself up in bed and requested the song, "I'll be shaking hands with mother in heaven." After hearing the song, he said, "Yes, that's what I'll be doing soon." He died that night. Sudden or violent deaths invariably call for a supernatural explanation in addition to their natural cause.

Funerals are the biggest social events of the neighborhood, more important in some respects than revivals. They are genuinely enjoyed, and they undoubtedly add color to the local life through their dramatic nature. Nowadays all families "belong" to one or another funeral home through burial insurance plans. When a death occurs, the mortuary concerned takes charge of the body, embalming it in town and returning it next day to a church on Big Smoky Creek below the burying ground now used by most Ridge families.

Funerals are usually held in the early afternoon, and they literally bring out everyone from miles around. Antagonisms are temporarily forgotten, although members of hostile families do not actually mingle with each other in the groups that start forming outside the church soon after dinner. The arrival of the hearse is the signal for the groups to move into the building as the coffin is wheeled to a point just in front of the pulpit.

Members of the family sit on the front benches, the men stoic but the women weeping loudly. Hymns are led by as large a group of singers as wish to gather on the platform at the front. The songs echo the familiar themes of death and heaven, a favorite being "When the roll is called up yonder." Then funeral sermons are delivered by as many preachers as could attend that day, each outdoing the others in praise of the deceased and most of them using the opportunity to warn sinners of their probable fate at death.

The high point of the service is not the preaching, however. It is the opening of the coffin after the sermons when everyone files past to view the body, the children being lifted by their parents so they can see, too. Members of the family are the last to go forward, and for them the thin scarf that has been draped over the face of the deceased is removed. This is the cue for emotional outbreaks of grief. Female relatives in particular may weep and shout, tell the virtues of the dead one, recall incidents in his life, and occasionally throw themselves across the coffin in a fit of hysterical weeping. These seemingly uncontrollable outbursts are in reality culturally controlled. They last the accepted length of time whereupon the individual, in a matter of seconds, becomes completely quiet and walks calmly back to her seat.

When all have taken leave of the loved one in this fashion, the coffin is closed, but not before a picture has been taken of the body. Pictures are taken later also at the side of the grave; they become treasured mementoes for the family. The trip to the cemetery begins, and the men have to carry the coffin on their shoulders up the last steep trail.

There are further prayers at the grave, and the lowering of the coffin is another signal for hysterical expressions of grief. The emotional displays dwindle as the grave is filled, and soon everyone is talking in normal tones, visiting and exchanging news. The funeral ends on an almost gay note of sociability as families begin to leave for home. They have gained strength to weather earthly trials in the reassurance of a heavenly reunion to come.

The supernatural sanctions described in the foregoing

pages make up the traditional religious base of Little Smoky Ridge. The values expressed through neighborhood churches, self-appointed preachers, revivals, and the occasional more intense movements are still deep and powerful. The desire to continue old religious forms is strong, but in this as in other affairs, the neighborhood has definite economic limits. Little Smoky Ridge does not today have a church of its own and it cannot afford the expense of regular protracted meetings. Its residents must rely on the facilities of more prosperous neighborhoods for their more expensive religious needs or go without.

The neighborhood would seem to have another alternative in the Mission chapel located in its midst, but Mission services have not proved to be an acceptable substitute for "real" religion. Many of the reasons for this state of affairs have little to do with religious forms as such. However, the differences between the Mission and local definitions of religion bear on acceptance or rejection of the chapel.

The circumstances leading to the organization of the Mission chapel in the late 1920s were not entirely foreign to local custom. The originator of the idea was an evangelical preacher from the region who at the time was finishing high school at Russell Cove. He felt a personal call to preach in the neighborhoods around the Cove and was soon taking a special interest in Little

Smoky Ridge. Preaching fiery sermons that stressed the imminence of the millenium, he gathered a large enough following to make him press for a church building.

At this point he encountered the factionalism between family groups and the waning enthusiasm after intense religious excitement. When the subject of a church was broached, "some wanted it, some didn't." Had the movement been strictly native, it would probably have died without leaving any tangible sign of its presence. In this instance, however, the preacher could call on funds from outside the region through the Mission at Russell Cove. Only minimum local assistance was needed, and this was pledged. The Brutons gave land and others promised labor and materials. Typical disagreements arose over redemption of the pledges, and each of the the two major family groups claims to have given more than its share while the other is accused of cheating on its obligations. Still, the first preacher seems to have held a sizeable congregation during the three years he was the pastor.

Differences have increased through the years as the central Mission at Russell Cove has supplied a succession of workers to fill the charge. At times these have been ordained ministers who served the Mission's four or five other charges also. As often, they have been teachers and other personnel assigned at random to conduct Sunday school in a number of neighborhoods, including Little Smoky. The rapid turnover of Mission personnel and the fact that workers see the people they work with only once a week or less operate against the establishment of effective working relations. Even more important are the wide differences in religious background.

While some of the workers assigned to Little Smoky Ridge have been products of similar cultural backgrounds, the majority have come from towns and cities in the Northeast or Middle West. They belong to one of the denominations that was originally highly successful on the frontier, but in the urban centers of the country their denomination has developed forms very different from those of its Colonial origins.

The Mission religion as it now enters the region represents the major changes that have developed in American Protestantism over two centuries of growing and adjusting to a complex industrial civilization. It reflects the trend toward rational interpretation of the Bible and a translation of religious experience into social action. It preaches good works and duty to fellowman as much as faith and allegiance to God. It also professes a general optimism about the perfectability of society through man's own efforts. Furthermore, the Mission denomination actively discourages emotionalism.

The religious background of workers from other parts of the country thus does not equip them to understand or sympathize with the religious behavior of Little Smoky Ridge. Moreover, they often come into the area with the same kind of missionary spirit that takes some of their fellow co-religionists into foreign fields determined to teach the natives "better ways" which means, of course, *their* ways. They are shocked at what they find, and few remain long enough to see more than the surface of the culture. Not appreciating or approving the local religion, they make no attempt to discover points of agreement between their own and the neighborhood's religious values.

Even when they know the values of their church are not understood, the missionaries are likely to be too committed to their denomination to change. Communion, for example, is celebrated periodically in a prescribed ritual which includes, among other unfamiliar forms, a long responsive reading. The minister is fully aware of the limited literacy of the congregation but includes the passage in its entirety, setting a pace too rapid for any of the members to follow.

Many of the points of variance are minor, and individual workers are able to minimize them. Their Sunday school classes are well attended and enjoyed, but they are not equated with "real" religion. The central purpose of religion continues to be defined differently by the two groups. The Mission sees the mark of religion in virtuous living and so emphasizes ethical behavior in all social relations. For Little Smoky Ridge the mark is still salvation which can only be achieved in an intense emotional experience.

CHAPTER EIGHT

A Frontier Folk in Transition

IN THE COURSE OF SEVERAL GENERATIONS SETTLERS IN the more remote parts of the Southern Appalachians developed the distinctive ways of adjusting to the physical, social and supernatural environment that have been described in previous chapters. Undisturbed by outside influences, they blended eighteenth century European backgrounds with American Indian practices in a simple technology well adapted to frontier conditions. The intimate personal world of family and neighborhood became the basic social unit, and ties with formal institutions had no compelling force. Nature, human nature and supernature as defined by the culture could be comprehended and handled personally by each individual or family.

Through continued isolation, the world of the Southern frontier became a folk world of small, isolated, homogeneous societies with a simple and almost self-sufficient economy.[1] In such societies there can be little occupational specialization or differentiation of roles beyond those of male and female, adult and child. Kinship provides the framework for ordering all activities and relationships. Members know each other as total personalities through long association and through sharing a common body of knowledge. Geographic and social isolation prevent the learning of other ways and facilitate the continuation of local ways.

Since folk peoples are largely non-literate all learning is by word of mouth and action. There is no storing of past knowledge beyond the memory of the oldest members. Each man's knowledge is the accumulation of his own lifetime, and life consists of growing into traditional ways that change so slowly as to seem fixed and unchanging. The old have relatively great authority by virtue of their longer experience, for the young are merely repeating the actions and experiences their elders have already been through.

In such a setting all activity has strong emotional overtones from being performed in the face-to-face intimacy of family life. Action acquires symbolic value as it expresses respect, loyalty and family solidarity in addition to meeting practical needs. All relationships in the natural and supernatural as well as in the social environment have a highly personal quality. Folkways develop and become entrenched as recurrent life problems are met in the same way by all members of the society through many generations. The traditionalized ways are accepted without serious question by each new generation; they become an integrated cultural system for meeting all needs.

Actual societies, of course, never completely fit the ideal picture of a folk society. Certainly Little Smoky Ridge is not entirely folklike. Yet its most distinctive qualities are the result of folk processes continued through half a dozen generations of little contact with outsiders. Here more than elsewhere in the United States all major experiences occur within the family where kinship supplies an emotional dimension to all activity and defines the authority of old over young and male over female. Kinship also provides the pattern for the development of neighborhood factions. In a world of personal relations there can be no neutral ground, and families must be either "for" or "against" participants in any quarrel.

Ways that were only temporary expedients on other frontiers here became folkways. Repeated generation after generation in the absence of alternative ways, they have become guiding principles, sacred in themselves and not to be questioned. Thus tradition defines as right and proper customs by which it is manifestly impossible to make a living at the present time. The tradition of the hunter, woodsman and patch farmer holds the men to a daily and seasonal routine that is ill-adjusted to commercial agriculture or a clock-regulated industrial system.

Within their own culture all are familiar with most of the available knowledge. The only major differentiation of roles is between "man" and "woman," although some may in addition be "preacher," "grannywoman" (midwife), or "conjure doctor" by virtue of possessing more of certain kinds of folk knowledge than their fellows. Some may also be millers or storekeepers, but these are usually only part-time and not necessarily permanent specialties. In all matters the organization for living is simple. The goal of life is perpetuation of old forms rather than a search for new ones. There is a unity of man with time and nature in a world which should be unchanging but which all in the present generation know to be in fact changing rapidly. Their culture provides no general principles for adapting to changed conditions, however.

In feature after feature Southern Appalachian culture has folk characteristics, as many have noted. Ballad collectors, folklorists, linguists, artists and novelists in particular have described the folk culture of the region in considerable detail. Much less attention has been given to analysis of the underlying conditions that encouraged the formation of something approximating a folk society in this region.

Along most American frontiers, including the Southern Appalachian one, conditions ordinarily prevented the full crystallization of a folk society. Even far back in the mountains the little communities seem never to have become self-conscious unified societies of the sort often associated with folk peoples. Too many factors combined to rush most parts of the country into a new kind of civilization. Existence on the edge of settlement only temporarily plunged families into isolation and adjustment by simple folkways. Most pioneers retained an image of the older society from which they had come. Everywhere, they tried to transform the wilderness as quickly as possible into a semblance of that society, especially in regard to the institutions of government, commerce, religion, and education.

In taming and populating each successive frontier, settlers moved rapidly from crude adjustments to complex civilization. In the fever of westward expansion there was little opportunity for small, isolated, homogeneous communities to become established. Events moved swiftly to connect new settlements with old in a network of communication lines and formal machinery for social control. Moreover, the population was far too mobile in their gamble for success in the new territories to form long-lasting ties with particular localities.

Only in the more remote sections of the Southern Appalachians and in parts of the rural South did settlements remain sufficiently isolated to become the kind of integrated social and cultural systems associated with folk peoples. How far the region moved in the direction of insulated self-sufficiency with a simple technology, family-centered social organization, and a sacred world view has been detailed in earlier chapters. Suffice it to say here that the region went its own way after being separated from the rest of the country.

However, the way that it went was the special way of the American pioneer fringe, a fact that has made for a shifting social world in a homogeneous cultural world. That is, men accepted and even preferred the wilderness environment in general without becoming permanently attached to specific localities or to specific persons other than their own families. Willingness to move to what might prove greener pastures in the next valley or on the other side of the mountain was part of the cultural pattern, and crude farming practices and soil exhausting crops hastened such moves.

Other values also operated against the forming of close associations with neighbors. The frontiersman could and would take care of himself, and his neighbors might do the same. The resulting regional picture is one of numerous, diffuse, shifting, and non-nucleated societies.[2] These are the "open-country neighborhoods" that began to appear first in the Middle Colonies and spread from there to the Appalachian frontier and later to the Middle West. While this settlement pattern was eminently suited to the necessities of the American frontier, it had its origin in the Old World and so was not entirely a product of the frontier.[3]

The fact that Little Smoky Ridge must be called a neighborhood instead of a community, and that its boundaries cannot be precisely defined, reflects the fluid nature of this type of society. There is a tendency for neighborhood groupings to shift their alignment as families move in or out or alter their relations with other neighborhoods. All the families included in the present study acknowledge residence "on the Ridge," but they may also at times designate more specifically "on Morgan," "up Rocky," or one of the other natural valleys that comprise the total neighborhood. Some of the geographic segments now united as Little Smoky Ridge have in the past been incorporated in different neighborhoods. The only constant organizing principle for contiguous topographic areas is kinship, and the present families of Little Smoky Ridge do not think of themselves as a cohesive social unit.

The continual disintegration and reformulation of neighborhood lines has probably accelerated in recent years, but the process is old. A sparse population has been distributing itself in scattered homesteads over a wide area of broken terrain for more than a century and a half. Large families and soil-depleting agricultural practices have necessitated constant shifting and redistribution of population. The settlement pattern has been one of shifting neighborhoods temporarily identified geographically with this or that branch of a watercourse and socially with this or that family. Several families might unite for mutual assistance at a neighborhood "working." Families have also united from time to time in maintaining schools and churches which perhaps tended to anchor some neighborhoods more permanently, although these institutions were likely to be almost as shifting as the population.

In fact, schools, churches and the like underwent the same simplifying process as the rest of the culture. Such extra-familial arrangements as remained became part of the informal, personal world of neighborhoods where frontier conditions persisted. Given the scattered population and the individualistic motives of most early settlers in the region it was impossible to transplant formal institutions from the older states. In places remote from expanding commercial and political centers the next generations also found the problems of basic survival more pressing than other concerns. Eventually generations in the deepest parts of the mountains grew up ignorant of anything beyond family life and the informal co-operative or antagonistic relations with other neighborhood families.

The few formalities of the outside world that accompanied the spread of population up mountain creeks and branches became attenuated and also personalized. Government and law, for example, sometimes reached far back into the region but most of the time officials have found it easy to ignore isolated settlements. Where officialdom does touch neighborhoods like Little Smoky Ridge it is interpreted in personal rather than abstract

terms. Government cannot be divorced from local politicians who win or lose votes on the basis of face-to-face
relations. Government also means taxes, the army, or
welfare agencies, but only as these personally affect local
lives. Similarly, formal law is something to flout when
it runs counter to customary whiskey making or hunting habits, but it is a valued tool when it can be turned
against a neighbor in a grudge fight. For the most part,
tradition condones informal enforcement of the mores.
Inter-family hostilities are usually handled by the families involved even when there is violence. The families
concerned may call in the "law," but no one else will.

Just as government and law became attenuated, informal and personal under continuing frontier conditions so did other institutions. Formal education, which
had not been overly important for the masses in the older
states, disappeared entirely in some parts of the mountains. In other places neighborhoods provided short
term "subscription" schools when they could afford to
and when some literate person desired to teach. School
was distinctly secondary to other pursuits, an occasional
luxury and not a necessity. The more important training for life was exclusively a family concern in which
children absorbed the skills and values of their parents
and prepared to repeat the cycle of marrying early,
building a home, clearing land, and raising a family. Occasional "singing schools" where itinerant singing teach-

ers taught part-singing by the shape note method seem to have been more popular and better attended than academic schools.

Religion also lacked formal organization as it fitted into the folkways of frontier society. The intensely Protestant and evangelical beliefs of the early Methodists and Baptists prevailed. These blended with a generally sacred view of man's position in a mysterious world governed by many supernatural forces beyond the control of humans. Heaven and Hell, God and Satan were fundamental realities with which each individual must come to terms. But religious needs could be met with a minimum of formal church organization.

Thus, in all respects the relatively simple institutions of eighteenth and early nineteenth century civilization became even simpler on the frontier. In remote districts the original adjustments to wilderness life became entrenched as new generations lived in intimate contact with relatives and had only few and impermanent relations with exponents of any other cultural system. Folkways became the guiding rules for many Southern Appalachian communities and they remain important today in some places. In addition to folk qualities, however, there are class distinctions which are also important in determining the social and cultural position of neighborhoods like Little Smoky Ridge. Both class and folk characteristics are present, and in recent generations class criteria have been gaining at the expense of folk criteria.

The key to social distinctions and to the whole process whereby some parts of the region became folklike and are now changing again toward contemporary American culture or else falling by the wayside lies in the distribution of population through time and space. A number of early travelers and later observers have recognized three distinct social classes in the region. Perhaps a better representation of the actual situation would be a continuum from moderately prosperous, commercially-oriented farms through smaller subsistence units to submarginal holdings. In general, since the earliest period of settlement the more prosperous yeoman class has been associated with the broader, more accessible, and more fertile lower valleys. A somewhat smaller class of poorer but still independent yeomen are to be found along the higher, less accessible valleys and coves and on some ridge lands. There are also dependent families in all sections, but proportionately they have been most in evidence on the remote ridges, especially since 1900.

The distinction between the social classes is real to people in the region. On the other hand, missionaries and social workers from the outside are inclined to lump the entire mountain population together, seeing "quaint" folk traits but also seeing "appalling" characteristics of a rural lower class. The effect of such discrepancies between outside and local views can be seen in the area below Little Smoky Ridge that is served by Russell Cove Mission. Church literature about the Russell Cove Mission resembles that of other mountain missions in picturing impoverished neighborhoods like Little Smoky as somehow typical of the region. And visitors to the Mission are shown the poorest and dirtiest homes since the Mission must justify its work to actual or potential outside supporters.

Local people have no such motivation and they resent the implications behind Mission actions. They draw lines that reflect the long standing social differences between ridge settlements and cove settlements. Families from the larger and more profitable farms "in the cove" and "down river" identify themselves with general rural middle class standards and feel superior to families "back on the mountain." Whatever their position was a generation ago they have gained in material wealth and modern conveniences and have more education than residents of the ridge neighborhoods. They are definitely oriented toward more developed regions, and it is a blow to be classed with people they themselves consider backward and primitive.[4]

There is a similar correlation between geography and social distinctions in the case of the presence or absence of folk elements, but the relation is more complex. In the whole region there is a range from a relatively unsophisticated brand of American urban life to the frontier folk society. These are roughly related to the more densely populated level areas and the sparsely populated rugged sections, respectively. They mark the extremes of communication with and isolation from other parts of the country. However, probably no more than half the 200 or so counties usually included in the Southern Appalachian region were ever sufficiently isolated for a long enough period to develop a folk society or an exclusively folk culture. Moreover, as the limits of possible expansion under "slash and burn" land clearing were reached an abrading process began to undermine the culture whether there was contact with the outside or not.[5]

Frontier technology in the absence of new lands was its own destroyer, and a time came in Little Smoky Ridge and similar settlements when a man could no longer solve the problems of soil depletion or providing for numerous heirs by acquiring more land. He no longer required the co-operation of neighbors to fell giant trees and roll logs from new fields. The necessary outlay in food for a house raising seemed more than the assistance was worth. So "workings" with their important social and recreational accompaniments disappeared. Families continued to be large, but acreage and crops became smaller. Living became increasingly difficult and families that had once lived amply by local standards dropped to marginal or submarginal levels. The neighborhood could no longer afford to support even the simple religious organizations it was accustomed to. The culture suffered reverses and abrasion in all aspects, not from any weakening of the integrating values but from sheer economic inability to express the values fully.

As cultural abrasion continued from internal causes, there were external forces to hasten the process. Isolation was beginning to give way before increasing inroads made by the outside world at the same time population pressure on the land was becoming acute. The introduction of commercial lumbering brought temporary relief in wages and compensation for timber rights to offset reduced production at home. Lumbering and other operations also brought increased participation in a money economy and greater awareness of what money could buy.

As the region opened, the greater availability of factory made and processed goods brought a decline in all folk arts. Machine-made cloth and finally ready-made clothes replaced homespun, and weaving disappeared except where it has been revived under outside leadership and a developing tourist trade. Furniture and household goods purchased at stores superseded hand-made articles—again except where a new handicraft industry has arisen. In like manner, folk music has given way to the popular "hillbilly" hymns and ballads. Today Little Smoky Ridge is a blend of old and new, folk and twentieth century American. The basic social framework is still relatively intact, but the outside with its social and cultural complexities is clearly here to stay, and the frontier folk society is passing.

CHAPTER NINE

The Outside Is Here to Stay

THE FAMILY AS THE BASIC MEDIUM IN WHICH THE individual learns the goals and values of his culture is still the center of Little Smoky Ridge's folk-like existence. By sharing a common value system and a common goal of perpetuating that system through the cycle of successive generations, the neighborhood continues to manifest a strong folk quality. So long as that unity of values remains, we are dealing with an essentially folk culture, even though there has been considerable modification of the material base: general impoverishment, substitution of factory made for homemade goods, and the like. Yet these are an emergent folk going through a period of instability.[1] Old ways are losing some of their importance through lack of the means to implement them. New ways are known through the continual presence today of the "outside," but there is neither the means nor any concerted desire to emulate them.

The ways and authority of other systems—legal, educational, military, medical, public and private agencies for social reform, and public opinion in general—can no longer be completely ignored or denied. The conforming process has begun, and ultimately Little Smoky Ridge must come to some kind of terms with the rest of American culture. The handwriting is on the wall, but so far the message does not mean the same to all who see it. Until neighborhood and outside share many more ways *and* means than they do at present, there will be friction and frustration between the two.

The public school and medical specialists are only two of many examples, but they may be used to illustrate some of the general problems involved when the neighborhood meets new social and cultural arrangements. It would be false, of course, to insist that the educational, medical, and other systems of the outside culture have left Little Smoky Ridge entirely unscathed, or that their effects will not increase fairly rapidly in the future. In the past, geographic and social isolation have somewhat softened their impact on the central structure of local society; but the American mass emphasis on consumer goods, omnipresent communication media, and universal education will no doubt eventually break the unified self-sufficiency of the family here as they have elsewhere. As others have suggested,[2] the social structure and ethos of folk peoples is often reached indirectly through their acceptance of the material wants of Western civilization while planned improvement pro-

grams that strike directly at deeply held values are being resisted.

By focusing on representative situations in which the
outside world and the neighborhood world meet along
a cultural frontier it is possible to see some of the strong
forces for conservatism in both. The outer world is,
after all, quite as unyielding in the process as the neighborhood, although Little Smoky Ridge is the primary
concern of these pages. The contact situations themselves may tend to increase the apparent conservatism
by engendering suspicion, distrust, and open resistance
to both persons and ideas from the other culture. Nevertheless, contact situations also throw into bold relief
mechanisms for stability and conservatism which are
always present but which may not be so obvious when
there is no external pressure.

Traditionally the frontier neighborhoods of the Southern mountains have met their educational and health
needs by folkways connected with the strong family
system. The more complex outside world meets such
needs principally by specialized knowledge associated
with systems outside the family, although the family is
expected to reinforce the educational and medical systems, and vice versa.

In most parts of the United States families expect to
adjust their routine to the schedule of a formal educational system. In Little Smoky Ridge the expectation,
or at least the wish, is for school terms to adjust to fam-

ily routine. The desirability of a little formal knowledge is generally conceded, but only so long as it does not interfere with the basic social and economic life of the family. Indeed, there is a certain tradition of formal schooling. It is the frontier tradition of the one-room, one-teacher school offering a little spelling, reading, writing and figuring. Terms were short and there were many years with no school at all. Eli Morgan recalls:

If I got three weeks' schooling, I called that *extra* good. We had to work a whole lot. There was fodder to pull, and one person couldn't do that alone. If he could've, the rest could have gone on to school. I told myself, "If I get to '*Baker*,' I'll count that good." Some of them spelled on through to "*Hospitality*." Webster's *Speller* was about the biggest book there was then. They finally brought in grammar, and that got some of them down. The schools weren't anything extra. The benches was just logs split in half with holes for the legs to fit, and you could pitch a dog through the cracks in the wall.

But first things came first; and planting, harvesting and other family work took precedence. Bad weather, poor roads and distance took a further toll of potential pupils. Even today most children in Little Smoky Ridge must walk at least half a mile to school. They are used to walking, but school is often defined as "too far" according to the social values which are more important than arbitrary units in measuring distance.

There is little awareness that changing conditions may require new kinds of knowledge, and parents do not encourage their children to go far in school. Families may attribute their present economic difficulties to anything from God to the government, and one occasionally hears the complaint, "I never went to school so I can't get no real easy jobs now." But that subjects learned in school could really help to improve their state is not seriously believed.

As a result of traditional ideas about schools and education not a single adult ever attended high school although for nearly thirty years there has been one less than five miles away. Nor are there any neighborhood children in high school at present. Only three adults have a seventh grade education. About 25 claim three to six grades, and about 15 are illiterate or only barely literate. Children of the present generation tend to feel "too big to be going to school" by the time they reach sixth grade, but there will probably be no complete illiterates in their group.

Actually there is little in local life to suggest a need for education. Since few occasions call for the skills of reading or writing, their lack is not felt. A storekeeper reads the occasional letters that come to the neighborhood, and there are usually two or three literate or semi-literate loafers at the store to witness an "X" on anything requiring a signature. Clerks at the county courthouse read and interpret whatever written notices the men need to understand, in fact, providing this service is an important vote getting device for county politicians. When a doctor gave Martha Bruton two kinds of white similar-appearing pills in identical envelopes, she solved the problem by marking one package with an "X." In other families school children do all the necessary reading and interpreting of the written word.

As for reading anything longer than directions on a bottle, it is a chore rather than a pleasure for most of those who are literate. Reading is not valued as a source of information or as a leisure time activity. Only one man reads a newspaper with any regularity, and one woman listens with pleasure to "human interest" items read to her by a friend in another community. Most families own a Bible and one or two other books as treasured but unread possessions.

Men who have worked outside the region might be expected to see more value in education, but if anything they are more inclined to consider it useless and unnecessary than the women who remain at home. Their interpretation of their experiences apparently does not suggest any need for change. For one thing they are not inclined to blame any lack in themselves for difficulties they may encounter in the outside world. Their early conditioning to an unquestioned position of superiority in the family inclines them to blame others before themselves. Also, verbal rather than written instructions are characteristic of the kind of laboring jobs they get.

Finally of course, exposure to the outside does not

insure an understanding of its values. The men take
with them a world view formed in their childhood environment. They can describe and discuss in realistic
detail the places, people and activities of mountain communities like their own. Their intimate understanding
of that cultural system then becomes the window
through which they interpret other cultures. They
simply fail to see many aspects of the new world they
enter. Many other aspects they reject. What they accept
is likely to reinforce beliefs already held as when a man
returned from the army more convinced than ever of
the literal truth of the Bible because in North Africa
he had seen the pillar of salt into which Lot's wife was
changed. Apparently the greater the gap between what
they know from their own world and what they see in
the other, the less likely they are to find a bridge between
the two.

The situation is changing somewhat among those who
have traveled and also among those who have never been
outside the region. A few persons express regret or em-
barrassment over their inability to read or write. The
feeling is situational, however, not chronic or even frequent. That is, a person asked to read something complains suddenly of poor eyesight, or the print is too small,
or he used to read a lot but is out of practice. Others
apologize for keeping all kinds of papers, books and
letters, "But when a body can't read he don't know
what might be important." Most simply ask someone

else to do their reading and writing for them, perhaps commenting, "My, wouldn't it be nice to know what all them words mean." The frustrations from illiteracy are still minor and are not translated into insistence that the children attend school.

Most parents more or less reluctantly send their children to the district school on Big Smoky Creek at the edge of the neighborhood. They voice much the same complaints about the school each year regardless of the particular teacher. The complaints include the distance the children must walk, the fights that occur on school grounds, doubts about the teacher, and questions about the value of the subjects taught.

A deeper, though less directly voiced, complaint seems to be against the interruption of customary routines by anything as inflexible as a school system. The school is the first agency to present a fixed, clock-determined schedule which clashes with local ecological-structural definitions of time. The school is not always the winner, nor does it ever win easily. Regular attendance is not valued, and children frequently stay home at their own or their parents' instigation.[3]

The struggle begins every summer as the question of enrollment arises. Tennessee law provides that no school may open for fewer than 25 pupils and also that children living more than a mile and a half from school cannot be forced to attend. Since most of the land south of Big Smoky Creek is uninhabited park land, there are years when there are not enough families with children in the district to assure the holding of school unless a few parents beyond the legal distance promise to enroll their children. The moving of one family in or out of the district just before a school term may necessitate rapid reshuffling of plans.

Under the circumstances, county teachers are not eager for assignment to Big Smoky, and the Board of Education may have to certify anyone they can find at the last minute. Teacher turnover has been great and their training and qualifications extremely varied. In 1949-50, for example, no one knew until the week for school to begin whether Big Smoky would open or not. At last there seemed to be 25 pupils available, and a minister from the Middle West who had been associated with Russell Cove Mission accepted the appointment as teacher. Attendance fluctuated throughout the year. On some days there were more than the original 25 when small children followed older siblings to school and were allowed to stay. On other days there were decidedly fewer than 25 in attendance.

Children rarely attend school regularly before they are seven or eight years old—distance, weather, and their own desires being sufficient reasons to keep them home on many days. Mothers also keep the youngsters home for companionship through long days that might otherwise be lonely since the women usually stay so close to home. The same women may leave their children

alone while they go to the store or mill, but that is different from sending the children away to school for a
stipulated number of hours each day. Family routine
also keeps older children home at times to help with
fieldwork or housework. Or sickness in the family may
be the excuse as when all three school age Bruton children stayed home for ten days after their mother had a
miscarriage.

In the Big Smoky school, classroom organization still
resembles the "little red schoolhouse" tradition expected
by the neighborhood. That is, one teacher instructs the
25 or more pupils who range in age from six to fifteen
and in grade from the first through the seventh. But
the curriculum and textbooks, as set by State and
County, present an unfamiliar world to the children.
Hygiene chapters assume the presence of running water
and other modern conveniences. A science lesson illustrates convection currents with furnaces and steam ra-
diators, but people in Little Smoky Ridge know only
wood stoves and fireplaces. There is little relation between the books and the rural reality in which the children live. Adding to the difficulty of unfamiliarity is
the feeling that all studying and reading should be confined to school hours. Home is *not* the place to prepare
for school.

So the children learn only what they can absorb in the
one room with its one long blackboard and its assortment
of old desks. The school has changed some from an older

one the parents remember. There, "We all sat close together on one long bench, and the teacher hit you with
his pointer if you turned your head." Today the teacher
"calls books" in a larger room with separate desks, and
he carries no pointer. So long as the children are reason-
ably quiet he works with each grade in turn and pays
little attention to the others.

The teacher assigns words for the second and third
graders to learn while the fourth and fifth graders work
sums at the blackboard and he takes the older grades to
the back of the room for a reading lesson. There is no
lack of respect for the teacher, but there is restlessness,
inattention and lack of interest. The younger ones actually do study for a few minutes before beginning to
fidget, and the somewhat older ones seriously add a few
columns of figures before starting to draw pictures.
Then the room breaks quickly into whispering and the
movement of trips to the pencil sharpener or to the
bucket for a drink of water. The older children in their
turn to study are somewhat quieter but spend the time
combing their hair or looking out of the window.

In imposing its rules of discipline and regularity the
school holds local activities in abeyance for brief periods,
but they soon reassert themselves. At recess the children
relax at once into customary male-female and inter-
family behavior. The sexes separate, and the boys are
apt to further separate according to the friendly or hostile relations between their families. All of the girls,

however, usually talk quietly together on the school steps. The boys soon initiate the teasing that so frequently characterizes relations between the sexes by throwing twigs at the girls and commenting about their boyfriends while the girls giggle and pretend to ignore them.

The smaller children are dismissed at the afternoon recess, but they usually wait for older siblings. Boys who are no longer in school also begin to appear at this time in anticipation of courting the older girls. When school finally adjourns, the group starting home may consist of thirty or more young people all teasing, courting or fighting as they head up the mountain. Smaller groups turn off at each side trail with the customary parting invitation, "Come, go home with us." The school has provided a convenient setting for the acting out of traditional roles while it is easy to forget the lessons taught there which have no immediate application to the local scene.[4]

The gulf between Little Smoky Ridge and the outside culture is even more striking in the field of health and medicine than in education. While formal school has always been a matter of indifference to the neighborhood, it at least has no systematic body of knowledge that runs counter to subjects taught in school, although the values placed on other activities prohibit spending much time there. On the other hand, the neighborhood does have an extensive body of medical lore accumulated through generations of isolation from formally trained medical specialists and practiced especially by certain "gifted" and "wise" old men and women who can advise their neighbors in any crisis. Their more or less systematic *materia medica* is a mixture of European folk belief, American Indian therapeutic measures, and patent medicine advertising, much of which is contrary to modern theories of disease etiology and treatment.

Remedies learned at home in the process of growing up have all the authority of strong family sanction. They seem reasonable because they are familiar and because everyone can cite many cures accomplished by them. Most scientific medical practices seem unreasonable and illogical, largely because they are unfamiliar and because they contradict local medical theory. Also, any procedure that calls for radical modification of habitual family routine is likely to be rejected in favor of the usual herb teas and long-accepted patent medicines that can be taken at home "as needed."

Most adults in Little Smoky Ridge recognize the symptoms and know treatments for a long list of common complaints not familiar to modern science. They take cognizance of vaguely defined maladies like "hives" and "bold hives," "phthisic" and other "lung fevers," "dew poison," "fall sores," "swelling" and "bloat." For each there are traditional home remedies as there are also for more obvious conditions like poison oak and snake bite. Families do also call on doctors, but more often as a last than as a first resort. And the fine distinctions made by State licensing boards go unrecognized where nineteenth century ideas still prevail. For example, people feel that old Dr. Carmer "ought to be training someone else now he can't get around." There have never been more than two or three licensed physicians to serve the entire mountainous eastern side of the county, and self-styled doctors often enjoy more confidence with the people than regular ones. In addition, various miraculous healers gain loyal supporters. Stories are told of men born with the "sign of the moon and the stars" on their chests who can cure merely by thinking about a patient whose symptoms have been described to them.

Medical personnel from a science-oriented culture therefore face a body of medical knowledge differing from their own and largely associated with the family system. They themselves represent a more complex society in which medicine has its own specialized content and its own organizational forms outside the family. They are as set and sure in their way as the neighborhood in its, and they tend to ridicule local beliefs. The two systems meet in such contexts as immunization clinics conducted by the Public Health Department and Russell Cove Mission and in individual cases where a family calls a doctor or where some contagious disease comes to the attention of health authorities.

The death, in 1950, of Julie Morgan from tuberculosis offers a particularly dramatic example of conflict between the systems, but the case is not extreme. In this instance the family never fully grasped the infectious nature of the disease as explained to them by a physician and at least two nurses, for germ theory is a far from obvious concept. The Morgans chose instead to accept a more general diagnosis by an unlicensed doctor in Holston who seems to practice a combination of chiropractic and folk medicine. His recommendations were more in keeping with local knowledge and they called for less modification of old habits than did those of the accredited physician who had originally diagnosed the case.

Throughout Julie's illness the family waited on her devotedly. If she wished to visit an aunt or a married brother on another branch, several members of the family accompanied her, waiting patiently as she paused frequently to rest. When she became too weak to walk, her brothers used their car, never complaining about damage done to it on trails meant only for foot or mule travel. In short, they did everything for her except insist that she obey the doctor's orders.

The physician, nurses, and other interested outsiders tried over a period of two years to place the girl in a sanitarium, but Julie's fears of the unknown and unfamiliar made her refuse. In this, the rest of the family backed her. They also felt that it was really a family duty to nurse her. At one time she did weaken long enough to consent to "try" the hospital, but within a

week the father brought her home. She had been home-
sick, and people at the hospital had been "mean"—that
is, they had insisted that she abide by hospital regula-
tions and schedules. Back home again, Julie spent the last
months of her life surrounded by solicitous relatives who
understood her needs and spared nothing to make her
comfortable. In the face of new medical notions and
an impersonal hospital organization she and her family
had found old ways more satisfying.

Other differences between modern health practices
and those of the neighborhood are not so pressingly matters of life and death, though they might result at any
time in fatal epidemics. Many attempts to institute immunization programs in the Southern Appalachian region have met with considerable success, for the nursing
profession has shown unusual ability in gaining the confidence of the mountain population.[5] Part of the work
is done through the public schools, but a series of clinics
held in Little Smoky Ridge in 1949 shows some of the
difficulties involved in reaching the whole population
of a district.

The clinics were organized by a nurse from Russell
Cove Mission in co-operation with the County Board of
Health primarily to give typhoid shots. Typhoid has
long been endemic in the area and is linked locally with
a variety of other "fevers," some mild and some serious.
Its specific nature and cause is not understood, and the
idea that it might be prevented by a shot in the arm is a

new one to the neighborhood and not fully credited. In this instance the nurse was fairly familiar with the culture and with local families. Knowing the conservatism and slowness to action of the people, she took every opportunity to discuss the clinic with them for several weeks before the first one was scheduled.

Talks began with Lige Floyd at his home on Rocky Branch during a regular "worming" session, for intestinal parasites are another chronic health problem. At least half the population harbor hookworms, roundworms, and whipworms much of the time. The Floyds could see no relation between the worms, polluted soil, and going barefoot, but the nurse had been making some progress. At least whenever the family heard the Russell Cove truck enter the hollow they scurried from the fields to the house to put on their shoes.

After giving out worm medicine and explaining the proper dosage for each member of the family, the nurse casually broached the subject of typhoid prevention. Lige, whose first wife and several of their children died from typhoid, ignored the topic. He continued a lively discourse on the weather, crops, and a recent trip to White City. The nurse let the matter drop after mentioning that the clinic would cost him nothing. On later visits, after apparently thinking it over, Lige informed the nurse that he was sure the shots would do no good, although he still did not commit himself completely.

At other houses few openly voiced any objections, and several expressed a feeling that the shots might be good for a number of ailments. None promised definitely to attend the clinics, but most said they might get to the Little Smoky church where they were going to be held. Finally even Lige allowed that the shots probably would not hurt anyone and his family might take them. The hesitancy to make any definite commitments or promises was part of a general pattern. The people rarely openly refuse to participate in programs planned by outsiders, but they do not like to be pressed for an answer before the actual event.

Naming a day and place for a socially valued event like a revival or a funeral will bring families together from all over the Ridge at approximately the appointed hour, but immunization clinics do not fall into the same category. In the end, the success of the program hinged on the nurse's willingness to make it mobile. The only families actually appearing at the church were the McCoys and Brutons who accepted a ride in the Russell Cove truck on the way up Rocky Branch. After they were treated, the clinic traveled from house to house on Roaring Branch and then returned to the Floyds on the first branch.

At each house there were initial excuses for not taking the shots that particular day. A few simply felt "too poorly." Others had work to do in the tobacco and feared sore arms would hinder them. Maggie Jones thought her grandchildren should have the shots, but of course they might not want them. In this as in most situations, the children made their own decision. When being brave through the ordeal became a game, most of the children complied amid encouragement and teasing from the adults. By the third week the shots were almost a ritual and even Lige Floyd began to talk as if he had favored the program from the first.

More than half the neighborhood residents are now temporarily protected, but their basic understanding of immunization practice has not materially altered. So long as clinics reach the neighborhood periodically the people will co-operate to the extent of rolling up their sleeves. But control of water pollution and other hygienic measures will probably await a time when increased desire for conformity to standards of the rest of the country indirectly brings improved sanitation.

In other matters pertaining to family health and welfare, also, there are differences between the neighborhood and the outside. Much of middle class American society relies on the findings and advice of specialists in matters that are still almost entirely part of the family system in Little Smoky Ridge. This is especially apparent in the area of maternal health and the rearing of children.

Childbearing, for example, is believed to be such a natural and inevitable function that it is not generally thought of as a matter for medical attention. Nor is it a matter for personal decision, although most adults seem to be aware of more or less effective birth control measures. All programs of planned parenthood have failed,[6] although the resistance to them may be passive just as it is for other health plans. In fact, in an abstract way, many of the women would like to be relieved of excessive childbearing and painful childbirth. The only action ever taken, however, is denial, as when one woman declared after the birth of a fifth child, "The name of this one is Quit" and sent her husband to sleep in another room. But for the most part there are insufficient pressures in the culture to make family limitation a positive value. In fact, the compelling values lie in the opposite direction since large families are central to the life of the society. The accepted roles for women are those of wife and mother. Since there are no alternative roles, a woman gains self-realization only through her position in a family.

In keeping with other parts of the culture the attitudes and practices at childbirth and through the early years of the children's development emphasize the exclusiveness and self-sufficiency of the family. There is scarcely more use of outside agents or specialized knowledge today than there was in past generations.[7] A physician is perhaps more often in attendance at a delivery now than in the past, although most women still call local midwives or have their babies "caught" by some older relative.

In every way, then, traditional customs practiced by the family in isolation from alternative systems make for continuance of old ways and a generalized, though often passive, resistance to new forms. Conditions are changing, but there is still little in the local culture to convey the idea of any necessity for change.[8] Neighborhood life flows along in relation to changing family situations and changing seasons, but the anticipation is that next year will be much like this year and last year. In this world of personal relations without written records and calendars or valued relations with outsiders, there is little inclination to compare present events with past events in such a way as to indicate the possibility of humanly controlled change. The familiar present, which is also the past and the future, provides the standard for judging all proposed changes.

When new ideas do appear, whatever their source, it can be seen that they strike the neighborhood in at least two ways. First, all ideas have a specific content according to the kind of factual knowledge they represent. Each new idea or set of related ideas becomes equated, where possible, with a corresponding body of local knowledge. Lack of knowledge in some specific area may make for nonacceptance of the new through indifference. Thus, the total unfamiliarity of subjects taught in school makes an unemotional rejection of them easy. On the other hand, where the neighborhood does have its own ideas in a particular field, rejection or acceptance of new concepts may be a function of their similarity or difference to local concepts. In this sense, the neighborhood resists new health practices that are contrary to its own medical theory.

But ideas do not occur in a social vacuum. They are tied to an organizational, or institutional framework which forms the second stumbling block for programs of change. In Little Smoky Ridge this organizational base is the family which is the system for carrying all social relations, knowledge and activity. By contrast, schools and medical specialists presuppose more or less formal social arrangements other than the family. They presuppose a facility in keeping appointments and submitting to arbitrary and impersonal rules of order.

Since the ability to relate oneself to others in a formal and nonsubjective manner is as much a part of learned behavior as is specific educational or medical information, new ideas face a double barrier. New ideas require modification in the content of culture. They also necessitate some rearrangement of family relations. The latter may be more difficult than the former to accomplish since family solidarity is learned very early, is constantly being reinforced through continuous interaction, and is so much a part of individual personality structure that it is not likely to be consciously questioned.

CHAPTER TEN

The Future

CHANGES OVER WHICH THE PEOPLE IN LITTLE SMOKY Ridge have little or no control are increasing in number, frequency, and intensity. The neighborhood cannot survive the inroads of time and the outside world much longer, and each year brings physical and social changes that alter neighborhood identity and rearrange its relations with other areas. Deaths have broken the direct continuity from the first settlers to present residents, and migration has removed other descendants of the original families and replaced them to some extent with floaters from elsewhere.

In several respects events since 1950 have tended to multiply the effects of isolation on Little Smoky Ridge. Most of Boone County has grown more prosperous from the booming tourist business which has by-passed the most remote neighborhoods for whom regional prosperity has come too late. Always on the outer fringe of developments, such neighborhoods are too poor to share in many of the opportunities of the tourist trade. They lack the means to provide goods or services directly although they can and do benefit indirectly from wages earned on roadbuilding and other construction projects. Tourist-serving occupations thus provide a new source of the non-farm income that has become so essential in recent generations.

On the other hand, development of the rest of the county has left Little Smoky Ridge more neglected by official attention than ever as it becomes less and less significant politically. The county road across the Ridge is more rutted and overgrown today than it was six years ago, and a new four-lane highway past Big Smoky Mountain has obscured several points of access to the neighborhood. Similarly, such ameliorative programs as Russell Cove Mission once supplied have almost ceased, since Mission support has lessened as the majority of the population of the area no longer needs or wants such services. Little Smoky Ridge is on the way to abandonment through oversight on the part of external agencies and through death and migration on the part of its own population.

It is impossible of course to know the exact form the abandonment process will take or to predict the response of individuals to the changing conditions. Yet if the record of the past is any indication, there are few alternative courses available to the present inhabitants. A review of past events in the natural history of the neighborhood suggests the limits for any future action.

Its geographic position, if nothing else, placed Little Smoky Ridge at the tail end of a settlement pattern begun in the Colonial period and pursued to its logical conclusion in the rugged remotenesses of the Southern Appalachian region. As the frontier complex of occupation, prodigal cultivation, and removal traveled farther up the steep valleys and ridges, the deteriorating effects of pioneer technology appeared more rapidly. At the same time, position far from market and trade centers prevented the early appearance of a more efficient technology that might have reduced the drain on soil and forest resources.

Its cultural position and the course of national history also contributed to the present situation of Little Smoky Ridge. For several decades there was relatively little difference between the Southern Appalachian population and the great masses of people in the Middle states, in the South, or in rural New England; but the seeds of later diversity were there. From the start the mountains were unattractive to certain social types. The New England town type of settlement was unsuited to the region as well as being culturally foreign to most of the first settlers; the same can be said of the Southern county form of settlement. Commercially minded farmers and entrepreneurs deliberately sought lands with greater profit potential and easier access to markets while a goodly number who preferred the life of the frontier hunter and patch farmer chose the fringe of settlement wherever they went.

Still, the large yeoman class of self-sufficing farmers

could be found in all the original states. Before the rise
of an exclusively money economy, mountain coves and
valleys were as attractive to this class as more open regions. Actually, until national expansion turned north-
westward and westward and until river and then rail
transportation supplanted transmontane routes, there
was as much communication through the mountains as
around them.

Until national developments turned away from them,
the mountain population shared the general culture of
many other rural and non-plantation regions. Only
later did the more isolated parts of the Southern Appalachians begin to acquire their distinctive ways which
so largely represented a retention of frontier customs
that had once been more widely spread over the country.
Within the region the population spread its special way
of adjusting to the world through numerous small and
separatistic neighborhoods. Scarcely touched by outside
events and trends, families wrested their living from
the resources at hand and did without schools, churches,
and formal government when necessary.

The final effect of continued isolation was perpetuation and even strengthening of the commitment to frontier technology, social organization and values long after
they had disappeared elsewhere. Well enough suited to
the wilderness environment originally, frontier methods
began finally to destroy the culture. Bottled up in remote mountain neighborhoods, frontier culture lost its

effectiveness, and a process of cultural abrasion began whether there was contact with other cultural systems or not. Large families practicing their primitive technology required more room for expansion than was available; and the steep slopes, limited soil fertility, and heavy rainfall of the region made continued working of old lands disastrous.

At about the same time, even the most isolated sections began to feel the need for more cash occasioned by the spread of the national economy into the region. By the end of the Civil War, internal and external factors were combining to force new adjustments. There was to be a decided lag, however, between the appearance of new economic conditions and the appearance of new customs to meet them. Old work habits, the simple division of labor within the family, and the informal nature of extra-familial institutions which allowed rapid adjustment on an expanding frontier became cultural handicaps when they continued to be guiding principles in situations requiring different adjustments.

Contemporary Little Smoky Ridge is the product of such clinging to outmoded ways, and the values supporting the old system still work against easy or rapid incorporation into a different way of life. Traditional patterns of land use insure an ever lower material level of living which further reduces the possibility of successful adjustment to modern American culture. At the same time, faith in a body of folk knowledge which accepts supernatural explanations for many phenomena makes for passive consent to conditions that would be unbearable for a more secular minded people convinced of man's ability to control and perfect his world.

At present, adjustment to the more secular outside world is thwarted by the local family system and the cultural world it imparts to its members. As long as the culture is almost entirely expressed and transmitted in a family setting, old values are likely to remain strong, for the very action of living and working together away from outsiders dramatizes and gives authority to the traditional culture. Full expression of the early ways may no longer be possible, but the steps to different ways are taken hesitantly and reluctantly. Practically everything valued in traditional family routine is at variance with the only available alternative, the largely impersonal and arbitrarily regulated culture of the machine age with its emphasis on technical proficiency. Little wonder that ventures into that other world do not effectively break the bond with the family-based world.

Increasingly, distance does break family ties in a physical sense, but it is the psychological attachment to family and to customary behavior that makes formation of new habits difficult. There has been out-migration from the neighborhood in every generation, much of it representing little or no psychological break with the past. Movement to the next county may bring as permanent physical separation from the childhood home as removal to a distant state, but movement to the next county usually means establishing a home like the original one and carrying on the activities that preserve a sense of family and cultural continuity. Migration to another part of the country, on the other hand, is likely to make the psychologically satisfying beliefs of a mountain upbringing suddenly useless as techniques for adjusting to reality. They may still be valuable as symbols of home and emotional security to sustain the individual in a strange and confusing world, but they offer few clues for accommodating to the new situation.

Nevertheless, for people in dead end neighborhoods like Little Smoky Ridge, migration to industrial centers may be the most logical choice in the future. This does not lessen the difficulties inherent in such a move. The experiences of migrants in the past call attention to the problems future migrants may expect, for the record of out-migration goes back more than fifty years.

At a time when wages in lumbering or mining were beginning to offer new economic hope to part of the Southern Appalachian population, others were joining the movement into Southern industry which was well along in its first boom stage by 1900. The mushrooming cotton mills of the Piedmont drew labor from the mountains as well as from coast and Piedmont. Today, many families have a longstanding habit of movement back and forth between Blue Ridge or Smoky Mountain farms and the Carolina mills.

While a good many who were originally lured out of the mountains returned, there was a fairly steady flow of labor into the mill villages to swell the ranks of the then new white working class of the South. In the villages, mountain families met workers from other areas who resembled them culturally to a large degree but who had lived under a different social system as tenants or sharecroppers in the old plantation regions before entering the mills. Together, they became a new Southern subculture, segregated socially and residentially from other whites and exhibiting both folk and lower class behavior.[1]

Except for the cotton mills, industrialization and urbanization proceeded slowly in the South. From World War I to 1930, migration from the Southern Appalachians turned northward to Akron, Detroit, Flint, Chicago, Cincinnati, Louisville, and other rising manufacturing cities. Since World War II, the South has again been attracting mountain workers to Asheville, Atlanta, Birmingham, Chattanooga, Knoxville, and other rapidly growing industrial centers.

Today, another industrial pattern, begun in the 1930s, has become well-established in the great valleys and right up to the edge of the mountains in the region. Many small plants and a few large ones have moved closer to the source of their mountain labor supply. The arrangement allows workers to combine factory employment with part-time farming on lands which are too small or too poor for commercial farms but which give the families a margin of safety in produce for home consumption. Little Smoky Ridge, of course, is a few miles beyond effective commuting distance from any industry. In this as in so many respects, regional prosperity does not quite reach the neighborhood; actual migration is necessary to obtain industrial employment.

In prosperous times a spontaneous erratic migration takes many into jobs in other regions, and the few local non-farm sources of income allow those who remain to struggle on. The depression years, however, showed how tenuous the hold of migrants to the outside is and revealed the extreme shakiness of the local economic base. Out-migration not only stopped, but thousands returned to the region that had never ceased to be "home." As a result, the Southern Appalachian region became the nation's largest problem area.[2]

It is precisely in neighborhoods like Little Smoky Ridge that migration takes on the aspects of a major emotional upheaval, for the ways there are least like those of the outside world and attachment to family and tradition is strongest. The lack of any strong drive for pecuniary gain or material possessions tends to keep potential migrants home. There is great reluctance to

make the final decision to leave, and the search for outside employment is postponed until drastic economic
need forces the issue. There is also the problem of separation, for most of the women are genuinely afraid to
leave their familiar surroundings. A man may have been
away on jobs many times before he can persuade his
wife to join him. She may then begin pleading to come
home almost at once.

Usually the man makes at least the initial trip alone
or with a few male companions after thinking about
the move for a long time. The final precipitating factor is likely to be a vague rumor that "they're taking
on hands" in Detroit or some other city. In the city, a
combination of cultural background and insufficient
funds penalizes the migrant. He rarely has more than
a general notion of where jobs may be available at the
moment, and he has even less knowledge of the proce-
dures most plants expect applicants to follow. Unskilled in either industrial trades or in organized community living, he is at a disadvantage in competition for
work or for a place in urban society.

The disadvantages are not completely insurmountable,
and many of those who began leaving the mountains in
the 1920s or earlier have been absorbed into the working
class or middle class segments of the communities to
which they moved, although certain retarding features
of their rural background tend to persist.[3] However,
studies made over the past twenty years show that per-

sons migrating since 1950 face almost exactly the same difficulties in becoming integrated as those who left before 1930.[4]

The process by which the newcomer from the mountains enters the urban social world parallels in many respects the assimilation of foreign immigrants, for in many Northern cities the "hillbilly" is as much an ethnic type as any European group and for the same reasons. Very commonly the man who sets out from a Southern Appalachian community already has friends or relatives or friends of friends in the city who are a first contact and source of job information. They also assist in finding a place to live which leads to the growth of residential areas that become stereotyped as "hillbilly" neighborhoods.[5] This type of association with others of his own kind plus continued orientation, and usually frequent visits, to relatives back home establishes a pattern of self-imposed isolation from other groups in the city. The sense of separateness is further reinforced by the attitudes and actions of other groups who accord a position of inferiority to the "hillbillies."

The urban experiences of people from the Southern Appalachians seem to have produced a more overt group consciousness and identity than ever obtained in their home communities, where interfamily antagonisms provide the spice of life. In a strange environment and in the face of prejudice, their cultural homogeneity provides a sufficient reason for mutual allegiance. Out-

siders easily note the characteristic dialect and cultural
mannerisms and react to the group as a whole regardless
of the many different parts of the mountains represented
by its members, and the individuals themselves are soon
reacting as members of a group. To the group, outsiders
generally ascribe such characteristics as "ignorance,"
"shiftlessness," "clannishness" and a "temperamental
streak," which, like most stereotypes, is a value-loaded
caricature with some basis in fact. The group makes of
its ethnic status a symbol of superiority rather than inferiority and fosters among its members myths of group
virtue. For example, they believe that employers consider their services extremely valuable and prefer them
to Italians, Poles, or other "foreigners."

In fact, the migrants from the Southern Appalachians
seem to pose a considerable problem to Northern employers who view them with mixed feelings. They are
an important and plentiful source of labor for the less
skilled manfacturing operations, but they are not always
amenable to industrial imperatives. Noting some of the
mountain characteristics, one employer writes:

From an industrial standpoint, this clannishness is both
an advantage and a disadvantage . . . with some of our
southern workers we have this separate allegiance, this
group loyalty to an unofficial leader. This leader has
no particular contact with either foreman or union. He
is not responsive to the motives or desires of either. Not
long ago, for example, we experienced a costly slow-
down in one department because a man from Tennessee,

the tacitly-appointed leader of a group of Southerners there, decided he did not like the way his department was being run.[6]

And in connection with other qualities:

. . . we have noticed a comparative lack of emotional stamina or persistence on the part of some southern workers. New employees from the South tend to become discouraged more quickly, to leave at the end of the first week or so of employment, to suffer imaginary backaches, than new employees from the northern cities.[7]

Over a period of years many eventually become accustomed to industries and cities and cease to visit the mountains, or are restless and dissatisfied when they do go home. Their children will grow up under urban influences and will probably have fewer deterrents to assimilation than the children of foreign immigrants since their physical characteristics are those of old American stock. Other migrants return to the mountains more or less permanently after frustrating and unsuccessful ventures into the outside world. For them, a certain bitterness may remain because of their experiences and it may increase their antipathy to any modification of behavior in the direction of meeting the demands of modern society.

In recent generations about half the children of Little Smoky Ridge families have left the immediate vicinity of Big Smoky Mountain, though not all of these have found their way outside the region or even into the more modern Southern Appalachian communities. The num-

ber leaving the neighborhood will almost surely increase
in the present and future generations, but at least some
of the houses will continue to be occupied for some
time to come.

Those who remain in the mountain region are facing
some of the same growing awareness of an ethnic position as their relatives in town, for the term "hillbilly" is
widely known. As a name for a special kind of popular
music the word evokes no particular reaction, but as a
label for a social type it has the same connotations in the
mountains as in other places. The actual influx of outsiders, especially tourists, and the ever greater awareness
of general American standards have brought increased
self-consciousness. Rather than unifying the mountain
population, however, consciousness of the implications
of the epithet in this instance has increased the social
distance between those whose desire is to conform to
national norms and those still practicing traditional patterns.

Other factors also tend to widen the cultural gap
between neighborhoods like Little Smoky Ridge and the
great majority of the Southern Appalachian population.
The very enterprises that have harnessed resources and
brought rapid industrial and agricultural expansion to
most of the region in the past 25 years have left other
sections more remote from potential development than
ever. Quite possibly this is a necessary by-product of
progress for a region that has suffered for so long from

overpopulation on lands made submarginal by its own cultural practices.

Whether the condition was unavoidably necessary or not, the fact remains that past events leave fewer choices for future action open to the Little Smoky Ridges than to other kinds of neighborhoods. Programs that required the public purchase of millions of acres of land, for example, have brought better flood control, improved navigation lanes, tremendous power potential, scientifically managed forests, the development of recreational facilities, and an increase in agricultural and industrial productivity to the region as a whole. Yet the purchase of lands around Little Smoky Ridge that furthered the program of the Great Smoky Mountains National Park left that part of the county with reduced incentive and fewer resources for providing schools, churches, farm to market roads, and other amenities than there had been before.

The story has been repeated many times by the Tennessee Valley Authority in its acquisition of reservoir lands. The Authority made far more elaborate plans for resettling displaced persons than is customary after learning how badly adjusted to their new locations and how dissatisfied with the treatment given them were the families removed from the National Park lands. However, the Authority made only minimum purchases at reservoir sites, and families on the surrounding lands that were rendered inaccessible by flooding were left to cope with the problem as best they could. The reservoirs covered the better bottom lands, reduced the size of many farms along the margins, and further fragmented individual holdings by embayments. Furthermore, no provisions were made for constructing access roads to the remaining farms; and counties which were also disarranged by the reservoirs have tended to ignore such remnant areas.[8]

The neglect of poor and isolated neighborhoods by county, state, and federal agencies is a long standing condition in the region. Test demonstration farm programs and agricultural extension work in general, for example, tend to ignore the small subsistence farmer on his remote ridge. They concentrate on the better-educated and more prosperous farmers who are already culturally and psychologically receptive to change. The agents naturally prefer to work where they can quickly point to substantial and concrete results. They are also apt to be under political and economic pressure to give their time and attention to dues-paying members of the county Farm Bureau to the neglect of the low-income farmer. The net effect is to increase the apparent differences between the ridge neighborhoods and others.

The extension of rural electric services has worked to the same end. Electricity has altered the homes and lives of many in the last twenty years, but getting power lines implies a certain amount of community co-operation, financial assets, and a large enough population to make

the service profitable. Little Smoky Ridge of course
lacks these and will probably never have electricity. Adjacent neighborhoods are just beginning to receive
power. As families along the creek install modern ap-
pliances the observable differences between their homes
and those on the Ridge will increase, and inequalities in
outward appearances promote feelings of deeper dispari-
ties.

It would seem that there has been a snowballing of
events and trends to place Little Smoky Ridge at a disadvantage in the contemporary world. Families who
continue to live there can only look forward to an extremely low-income form of farming with no regular
possibility of non-farm employment in the vicinity, at
least not in activities congenial to traditional habits.
Lumbering is not likely to revive on any large scale in
this particular section. Moonshining, which at present is
both lucrative and congenial, is likely in the future to
feel the effects of greater law enforcement as town
mores become more prevalent in surrounding areas. The
present boom in roadbuilding and construction projects
will slacken soon, and future crew foremen may not be
so lenient of local irregularity in reporting for work, for
the ways of the time-clock world are extending.

The final foreseeable future for Little Smoky Ridge
as a neighborhood is disintegration, which has already
begun, and finally death. There has been a continuous
decline in neighborhood integration for many years. Co-

operation in the form of "workings" disappeared long ago. Other activities also have declined as the means for supporting them have gone. The isolation of the separate households increases as families move away, and the ties that hold the rest to the neighborhood seem to be more ephemeral each year. The three or four elderly residents will probably live out their lives in the present setting. Families of "squatters" will continue to come and go for a while, occupying old houses and raising small crops on old lands for a season or two before leaving. The majority of the young people will probably find their way eventually into contemporary society either by gradual moves down the creek or by a sudden plunge into the outer world. Some of them will probably join the "squatters," but ultimately houses now occupied will become abandoned ruins like those that already dot the Ridge landscape.

Little Smoky Ridge has come late to a stage of disintegration passed earlier in many parts of the United States. The death of rural neighborhoods with their country stores, frame churches, and one-room schools is a phenomenon that typifies the great mobility of the American people and the unprecedented growth of an industrial civilization that spans a continent. The process became most pronounced in the great sweep of urban growth after 1920 when thousands left the farm for the city and the automobile began to make the farms themselves part of the city. But the movement had begun long before that, notably in the great exodus from the New England and upper New York hill country after 1870. Wherever and whenever settlers were caught by the shift from self-sufficiency to a money economy on lands unsuited for commercial production they soon deserted their farms for new lands or for town life. In much the same manner, the more remote parts of the Southern Appalachians are being abandoned today. The inhabitants face special difficulties stemming from their long isolation in a self-destroying frontier folk culture and their late re-entrance into the mainstream of American life. Individuals and families will undoubtedly catch up, but the Little Smoky Ridges, as neighborhoods, will perish.

Notes and References

CHAPTER II

1. David Crockett, *The Autobiography of David Crockett*, p. 101.

2. The Southern Appalachian region is defined geographically by C. W. Hayes, *The Southern Appalachians*; H. B. Ayres and W. W. Ashe, *The Southern Appalachian Forests*; L. C. Glenn, *Denudation and Erosion of the Southern Appalachian Region and the Monongahela River*; Isaiah Bowman, *Forest Physiography*, pp. 107-126, 603-706; N. M. Fenneman, *Physiography of Eastern United States*, pp. 84-134, 163-279, 329-337. In defining the region politically and culturally authorities include between 205 and 236 counties, often distinguishing 98 or 100 of these as "mountain counties." N. Frost, *A Statistical Study of the Public Schools of the Southern Appalachian Mountains*, pp. 7-29; J. C. Campbell, *The Southern Highlander and His Homeland*, pp. 10-18; U. S. Department of Agriculture, *Economic and Social Problems and Conditions of the Southern Appalachians*, pp. 1-6; R. B. Vance, *Human Geography of the South*, pp. 4-10, 27-36, 73-108, 240-260; J. S. Brown, "The Changing Highlands Population."

3. H. H. Bennett, *The Soils and Agriculture of the Southern States*, pp. 1-51, 167-212; C. A. Mooers, *Soils of Tennessee*.

CHAPTER III

1. Sources that bear especially on settlement of the Tennessee Valley and Blue Ridge-Smoky Mountain provinces include John Haywood, *The Civil and Political History of the State of Tennessee*; J. G. M. Ramsey, *The Annals of Tennessee*; E. C. Semple, *American History*

and Its Geographic Conditions, pp. 36-92; J. P. Arthur, *Western North Carolina;* S. C. Williams, *History of the Lost State of Franklin, Dawn of Tennessee Valley and Tennessee History, Tennessee During the Revolutionary War,* and ed. *Early Travelers in the Tennessee Country, 1540-1800;* T. P. Abernethy, *From Frontier to Plantation in Tennessee;* L. C. Gray, *History of Agriculture in the Southern United States to 1860,* pp. 85-93, 116-126, 438-489, 614-639.

2. Ramsey, p. 72.

3. This part of East Tennessee figured in the stormy political developments and counter claims of early Virginia, North Carolina, the Watauga Association, the State of Franklin, the United States Territory South of the River Ohio, and finally the State of Tennessee.

4. Present residents sometimes report that they have "rented" a house or farm. When asked how much rent they paid, the reply is, "Oh, we didn't pay anything; we just rented." I was unable to determine the exact local usage of the word "rent."

5. Mildred Haun, *The Hawk's Done Gone,* pp. 187, 189.

CHAPTER IV

1. F. J. Turner, *The Frontier in American History,* and *The Significance of Sections in American History;* G. R. Taylor, ed., *The Turner Thesis.*

2. The question of national origins of the present Southern Appalachian population is hopelessly tangled. Many volumes by historians and would-be historians deal at length with the Scotch (or Presbyterian) Irish, the English, the Germans and the French Huguenots who all had a part in peopling the region. Some writers insist the mountain population is "pure Anglo-Saxon," endowed only with virtues. Others would have them all the descendants of indentured servants or "criminals and worse." Probably they represented the same national and cultural origins and in about the same proportions as in the general population of all the Middle and Southern colonies.

3. Carl Bridenbaugh, *Myths and Realities*, p. 130f.

4. F. L. Owsley, "Patterns of Migration and Settlement on the Southern Frontiers," and *Plain Folk of the Old South*; Bridenbaugh, pp. 119-196.

5. David Crockett, *The Autobiography of David Crockett*, p. 101.

6. James E. Montgomery, *Three Appalachian Communities*, and "Three Southern Appalachian Communities; an Analysis of Cultural Variables."

CHAPTER V

1. J. B. Knox, *The People of Tennessee*, p. 60.

2. J. W. Patton, *Unionism and Reconstruction in Tennessee 1860-1869*, p. 22.

3. C. D. Warner, *On Horseback*, p. 74f.

4. E. C. Case, *The Valley of East Tennessee*, p. 12.

5. Case, p. 13.

6. H. B. Ayres and W. W. Ashe, *The Southern Appalachian Forests*; R. C. Hall, *Preliminary Study of Forest Conditions in Tennessee*; Isaiah Bowman, *Forest Physiography*, pp. 107-126, 603-706; Mary Verhoeff, *The Kentucky River Navigation*, pp. 182-205; E. H. Frothingham, *Timber Growing and Logging Practice in the Southern Appalachian Region*; Stanley Horn, *This Fascinating Lumber Business*, pp. 17-48, 95-122.

7. Frothingham, p. 8.

8. Hall, p. 9f.

9. E. V. Brender and E. Merrick, "Early Settlement and Land Use in the Present Toccoa Experimental Forest."

10. R. E. Murphy, "A Southern West Virginia Mining Community"; M. Ross, *Machine Age in the Hills*; B. Crawford, "The Coal Miner," in W. T. Couch, ed., *Culture in the South*, pp. 361-373; U. S. Department of Agriculture, *Economic and Social Problems*, pp. 1-6, 39f., 120-127, *passim*; P. F. Cressey, "Social Disorganization and Reorganization in Harlan County, Kentucky."

CHAPTER VI

1. E. E. Evans-Pritchard, *The Nuer*, pp. 94-138.

2. Most families have a clock on the mantel, more for ornament than use. One of the few times I saw Lily Morgan's clock running, she had wound it specifically to keep track of the time for her husband's doses of "Back medicine," and it did not register the correct hour.

3. My statements are not backed by time studies, but several such studies lend quantitative support to the impression that members of simple societies devote as much energy and as many total hours to work as workers in industrial societies. W. D. Nicholls and J. H. Bondurant, *Farm Management and Family Incomes in Eastern Kentucky*, pp. 28-36; M. J. Herskovits, *Economic Anthropology*, pp. 88-89; C. J. Erasmus, "Work Patterns in a Mayo Village."

4. Talcott Parsons, "The Kinship of the Contemporary United States."

5. For descriptions of the special family form that has persisted in Southern mountain regions see J. C. Campbell, *The Southern Highlander*, pp. 123-151; Nora Miller, *The Girl in the Rural Family*, pp. 15-38; C. C. Zimmerman and M. E. Frampton, *Family and Society*, pp. 153-295; Claudia Lewis, *Children of the Cumberland*; F. D. Alexander and R. E. Galloway, "Salient Features of Social Organization in a Typical County of the General and Self-Sufficing Farm Region"; P. F. Cressey, "Social Disorganization"; J. S. Brown, "The Conjugal Family and the Extended Family Group," *The Farm Family in a Kentucky Mountain Neighborhood*, and *The Family Group in a Kentucky Farming Community*.

6. Brown, "The Conjugal Family."

7. This statement does not necessarily contradict the findings of personality studies that indicate a pessimistic and negativistic world view in several Tennessee mountain communities. There can be security and assurance in pessimism which here is closely related to the religious beliefs discussed in Chapter Seven. M. T. Matthews, *Experience Worlds of Mountain People*.

CHAPTER VII

1. C. C. Cleveland, *The Great Revival in the West, 1797-1805;*
E. R. Hooker, *Religion in the Highlands;* J. G. Leyburn, *Frontier
Folkways,* pp. 192-203; W. W. Sweet, *Religion in Colonial America,*
pp. 245-318, and *Religion in the Development of American Culture,*
pp. 98-159.

2. E. R. Hooker, "The Church Situation," in U. S. Department of
Agriculture, *Economic and Social Problems,* pp. 168-182.

3. The pervasiveness of religious and more broadly supernatural
values in everyday life has been noted by most observers of Southern mountain life. See J. C. Campbell, *The Southern Highlander,*
pp. 176-194; M. T. Matthews, *Experience Worlds;* Vance Randolph,
Ozark Superstitions.

CHAPTER VIII

1. Different investigators have defined folk societies and folk cul-
tures in various ways. Despite considerable controversy over details,
the concepts remain useful for assessing non-industrial societies.
H. W. Odum, "Notes on the Study of Regional and Folk Society";
Robert Redfield, *The Folk Culture of Yucatan,* "The Folk Society,"
and "The Natural History of the Folk Society"; Sol Tax, "World
View and Social Relations in Guatemala"; Horace Miner, "The
Folk-Urban Continuum"; G. M. Foster, "What Is Folk Culture?";
A. R. King, "A Note on Emergent Folk Cultures and World Culture
Change"; F. W. Voget, "The Folk Society—An Anthropological
Application."

2. R. Redfield, *The Little Community,* p. 6f.

3. C. M. Arensberg, "American Communities."

4. Cf. J. S. Brown, "Social Class, Intermarriage, and Church
Membership in a Kentucky Community."

5. Redfield has used the very apt expression "abraded culture" in
connection with another Southern Appalachian study of remote
neighborhoods in Virginia which show many parallels to Little

Smoky Ridge. Redfield, *The Little Community,* p. 6; Mandel Sherman and T. R. Henry, *Hollow Folk.*

CHAPTER IX

1. A. R. King, "A Note on Emergent Folk Cultures and World Culture Change."

2. R. L. Beals, "Notes on Acculturation," in S. Tax, ed., *Heritage of Conquest,* pp. 225-232.

3. The relation between the traditional family life with its cultural values and school attendance is brought out either directly or indirectly in studies of school conditions in the Southern Appalachians. N. Frost, *A Statistical Study of Public Schools;* O. L. Hatcher, ed., *A Mountain School;* W. H. Gaumnitz, "Schools and Education," in U. S. Department of Agriculture, *Economic and Social Problems,* pp. 95-119, and *Education in the Southern Mountains;* Claudia Lewis, *Children of the Cumberland;* W. T. Gray, "Factors Affecting Teacher Tenure in the Appalachian Highlands."

4. Some of the studies of Southern Appalachian children based on intelligence tests have failed, I believe, to take sufficient account of the difference between school knowledge and the kind of knowledge by which the children live in their own environment. N. D. M. Hirsch, "An Experimental Study of the East Kentucky Mountaineers; a Study in Heredity and Environment"; Mandel Sherman and C. B. Key, "The Intelligence of Isolated Mountain Children"; M. Sherman and T. R. Henry, *Hollow Folk;* L. R. Wheeler, "The Intelligence of East Tennessee Mountain Children"; E. J. Asher, "The Inadequacy of Current Intelligence Tests for Testing Kentucky Mountain Children."

5. Ernest Poole, *Nurses on Horseback;* E. L. Tiffany, "Selling Health in the Mountains"; Mary Breckenridge, *Wide Neighborhoods.*

6. Lena Gilliam, "A Contraceptive Service for Mountain Women"; G. W. Beebe, *Contraception and Fertility in the Southern Appalachians;* G. W. Beebe and M. A. Geisler, "Control of Conception in a Selected Rural Sample."

7. J. L. Hills, C. E. Wait, and H. C. White, *Dietary Studies in Rural Regions in Vermont, Tennessee, and Georgia;* F. S. Bradley and M. A. Williamson, *Rural Children in Selected Counties of North Carolina;* Lydia Roberts, *The Nutrition and Care of Children in a Mountain County of Kentucky;* Glenn Steele, *Maternity and Infant Care in a Mountain County in Georgia.*

8. Cf. H. G. Barnett, *Innovation,* pp. 56-64.

CHAPTER X

1. M. A. Potwin, *Cotton Mill People of the Piedmont;* Lois Mac-Donald, *Southern Mill Hills;* J. J. Rhyne, *Some Southern Cotton Mill Workers and Their Villages;* B. F. Lemert, *The Cotton Textile Industry of the Southern Appalachian Piedmont;* Liston Pope, *Millhands and Preachers;* H. L. Herring, *Passing of the Mill Village.*

2. P. G. Beck and M. C. Forster, *Six Rural Problem Areas: Relief-Resources-Rehabilitation,* pp. 9-11, 77-79, 94-97; U. S. Department of Agriculture, *Economic and Social Problems;* T. J. Woofter, Jr., "Rural Relief and the Back-to-the-Farm Movement"; Carter Goodrich, et al., *Migration and Economic Opportunity,* pp. 54-123, 503-519, 592-659; L. S. Dodson, *Living Conditions and Population Migration in Four Appalachian Counties;* C. C. Taylor, et al., *Disadvantaged Classes in American Agriculture;* C. P. Loomis and L. S. Dodson, *Standards of Living in Four Southern Appalachian Mountain Counties.*

3. H. W. Beers and C. Heflin, "The Urban Status of Rural Migrants"; C. Heflin and H. W. Beers, *Urban Adjustments of Rural Migrants.*

4. G. G. Leybourne, "Urban Adjustments of Migrants from the Southern Appalachian Plateaus"; E. D. Beynon, "The Southern White Laborer Migrates to Michigan"; M. G. Caldwell, "The Adjustments of Mountain Families in an Urban Environment"; M. T. Buchanan, *The Migration of Workers from Tennessee to Michigan;* L. M. Killian, *Southern White Laborers in Chicago's West Side,* and "The Adjustments of Southern White Migrants to Northern Urban

Norms"; Cincinnati Mayor's Friendly Relations Committee, *Report of a Workshop on the Southern Mountaineer in Cincinnati.*

5. Several of the studies cited above point out that, although there are concentrations of "hillbillies" in some neighborhoods, the label usually implies a homogeneity that is not actually present. Also, the term "hillbilly" is applied to all Southern white industrial workers, many of whom are not from the mountains at all. There are definite cultural similarities between Southern Appalachian and other Southern migrants, and it is interesting to note that workers from many parts of the South have themselves accepted the unity implied by the common label. Clearly, they recognize that they are more like each other than they are like their Northern neighbors.

6. J. R. Hundley, "The Mountain Man in Northern Industry," p. 35f.

7. Hundley, p. 36f.

8. T. J. Woofter, Jr., "Tennessee Valley Regional Plan"; M. H. Satterfield, "The Removal of Families from Tennessee Valley Authority Reservoir Areas"; B. H. Luebke, "Problems Created by the Douglas Reservoir in East Tennessee."

Bibliography

THE LITERATURE ON THE SOUTHERN APPALACHIANS IS VAST AND varied, both in content and quality, and it would be impossible and probably pointless to attempt a complete regional bibliography. On the other hand, the relatively great interest of lay and professional people alike in the area merits a more complete listing of reference materials than has been available in the past. With that in mind I have tried to include, in addition to all works cited in the foregoing pages, most of the reputable studies of the region's social and cultural development. Except for a few special cases, I have arbitrarily excluded fictional works, linguistic studies, purely descriptive accounts of folk arts or folklore, and most references to the culturally related Ozark mountain region or other Southern subregions.

Abernethy, Thomas P. *From Frontier to Plantation in Tennessee.* Chapel Hill: University of North Carolina Press, 1932.

Alexander, F. D. and R. E. Galloway. "Salient Features of Social Organization in a Typical County of the General and Self-Sufficing Farm Region," *Rural Sociology,* 12:395-405. 1947.

Allred, C. E., H. J. Bonser and E. J. Lebrun. *Significant Changes in Agriculture of Cumberland County, Tennessee.* Tennessee Agricultural Experiment Station, Monograph 139. Knoxville, 1942.

Arensberg, C. M. "American Communities," *American Anthropologist,* 57:1143-1162. 1955.

Arnold, J. H. *Ways of Making Southern Mountain Farms More Productive.* U. S. Department of Agriculture, Farmers' Bulletin 905. Washington: Government Printing Office, 1918.

Arthur, John P. *Western North Carolina; A History from 1730 to 1913.* Raleigh: Edwards & Broughton, 1914.

✓ Asher, E. J. "The Inadequacy of Current Intelligence Tests for Testing Kentucky Mountain Children," *Pedagogical Seminary and Journal of Genetic Psychology*, 46:480-486. 1935.

Avery, M. H. and K. S. Boardman, eds. "Arnold Guyot's Notes on the Geography of the Mountain District of Western North Carolina," *North Carolina Historical Review*, 15:251-318. 1938.

Ayres, H. B. and W. W. Ashe. *The Southern Appalachian Forests*. U. S. Geological Survey, Professional Paper 37. Washington: Government Printing Office, 1905.

Beck, P. G. and M. C. Forster. *Six Rural Problem Areas: Relief-Resources-Rehabilitation*. Federal Emergency Relief Administration, Research Monograph 1. Washington: Government Printing Office, 1935.

Beebe, Gilbert W. *Contraception and Fertility in the Southern Appalachians*. Baltimore: Williams & Wilkins, 1942.

✓ ———— and M. A. Geisler. "Control of Conception in a Selected Rural Sample," *Human Biology*, 14:1-20. 1942.

✓ Beers, H. W. and C. Heflin. "The Urban Status of Rural Migrants," *Social Forces*, 23:32-37. 1944.

————. *People and Resources in Eastern Kentucky*. Kentucky Agricultural Experiment Station, Bulletin 500. Lexington, 1947.

Bennett, H. H. *The Soils and Agriculture of the Southern States*. New York: The Macmillan Company, 1921.

Beynon, E. D. "The Southern White Laborer Migrates to Michigan," *American Journal of Sociology*, 3:333-343. 1938.

Bondurant, J. H. and W. D. Nicholls. *Labor Supply and Farm Production on Eastern Kentucky Farms*. Kentucky Agricultural Experiment Station, Bulletin 475. Lexington, 1945.

Bowman, Isaiah. *Forest Physiography*. New York: John Wiley & Sons, Inc., 1914.

Bradley, F. S. and M. A. Williamson. *Rural Children in Selected Counties of North Carolina*. U. S. Department of Labor, Children's Bureau, Publication 33. Washington: Government Printing Office, 1918.

∨ Breckenridge, Mary. *Wide Neighborhoods*. New York: Harper & Brothers, 1952.

Brender, E. V. and E. Merrick. "Early Settlement and Land Use in the Present Toccoa Experimental Forest," *Scientific Monthly*, 71:318-325. 1950.

Bridenbaugh, Carl. *Myths and Realities; Societies of the Colonial South*. Baton Rouge: Louisiana State University Press, 1952.

Brown, James S. "The Social Organization of an Isolated Kenutcky Mountain Neighborhood." Unpublished Ph. D. dissertation, Harvard University, 1950.

──────. "Social Class, Intermarriage, and Church Membership in a Kentucky Community," *American Journal of Sociology*, 57:232-242. 1951.

──────. "The Conjugal Family and the Extended Family Group," *American Sociological Review*, 17:297-306. 1952.

──────. *The Farm Family in a Kentucky Mountain Neighborhood*. Kentucky Agricultural Experiment Station, Bulletin 587. Lexington, 1952.

──────. *The Family Group in a Kentucky Mountain Farming Community*. Kentucky Agricultural Experiment Station, Bulletin 588. Lexington, 1952.

∨ ──────. "The Changing Highlands Population," *Mountain Life & Work*, 29, No. 2:42-43. 1953.

────── and H. W. Beers. *Rural Population Changes in Five Kentucky Mountain Districts, 1943 to 1946*. Kentucky Agricultural Experiment Station, Bulletin 532. Lexington, 1949.

Buchanan, Margaret T. "The Migration of Workers from Tennessee to Michigan." Unpublished Master's thesis, Vanderbilt University, 1940.

Burns, Inez. "Settlement and Early History of the Coves of Blount County, Tennessee," *East Tennessee Historical Society Publications*, No. 24:44-67. 1952.

Campbell, John C. *The Southern Highlander and His Homeland*. New York: Russell Sage Foundation, 1921.

ᐯ Carothers, J. E. "Poverty Stalks the Small Farmer," *Mountain Life & Work*, 31, No. 1:17-19. 1955.

Case, Earl C. *The Valley of East Tennessee; the Adjustment of Industry to Natural Environment*. Tennessee Geological Survey, Bulletin 36. Nashville, 1925.

Clark, Blanche H. *The Tennessee Yeoman, 1840-1860*. Nashville: Vanderbilt University Press, 1942.

Clark, Elmer T. *The Small Sects in America*. New York and Nashville: Abingdon-Cokesbury Press, 1949.

Clayton, C. F. and W. D. Nicholls. *Land Utilization in Laurel County, Kentucky*. U. S. Department of Agriculture, Technical Bulletin 289. Washington: Government Printing Office, 1932.

Cleninger, W. R. "Southern Appalachian Highlanders in Western Washington," *Pacific Northwest Quarterly*, 33:3-25. 1942.

Cleveland, Catherine C. *The Great Revival in the West, 1797-1805*. Chicago: University of Chicago Press, 1916.

Cole, W. E. and S. E. T. Lund. "The Tennessee River Valley; its People, Resources, and Institutions," *Journal of Educational Sociology*, 15:130-136. 1941.

Combs, Josiah H. *The Kentucky Highlanders from a Native Mountaineer's Viewpoint*. Lexington: J. L. Richardson, 1913.

Couch, W. T., ed. *Culture in the South*. Chapel Hill: University of North Carolina Press, 1935.

Craig, R. B. *Forestry in the Economic Life of Knott County, Kentucky*. Kentucky Agricultural Experiment Station, Bulletin 326. Lexington, 1932.

✓ Cressey, Paul F. "Social Disorganization and Reorganization in Harlan County, Kentucky," *American Sociological Review*, 14:389-394. 1949.

Crockett, David. *The Autobiography of David Crockett*. New York: Charles Scribner's Sons, 1923.

Dargan, Olive T. *From My Highest Hill*. Philadelphia: J. B. Lippincott Company, 1941.

Davis, D. H. *Geography of the Mountains of Eastern Kentucky*. Kentucky Geological Survey. Frankfort, 1924.

————. "The Changing Role of the Kentucky Mountains and the Passing of the Kentucky Mountaineer," *Journal of Geography*, 24, No. 2:41-52. 1925.

————. "Study of the Succession of Human Activities in the Kentucky Mountains, a Dissected Highland Area," *Journal of Geography*, 29:85-100. 1930.

Day, John F. *Bloody Ground*. New York: Doubleday, Doran & Co., 1941.

Dodson, L. S. *Living Conditions and Population Migration in Four Appalachian Counties*. U. S. Department of Agriculture, Farm Security Administration, and Bureau of Agricultural Economics, Social Research Report 3. Washington: Government Printing Office, 1937.

Duerr, W. A., J. B. Roberts and R. O. Gustafson. *Timber-Products Marketing in Eastern Kentucky*. Kentucky Agricultural Experiment Station, Bulletin 488. Lexington, 1946.

————, et al. *Farms and Forests of Eastern Kentucky in Relation to Population and Income*. Kentucky Agricultural Experiment Station, Bulletin 507. Lexington, 1947.

Duncan, H. G. "Southern Highlanders," *Journal of Applied Sociology*, 10:556-561. 1926.

Eaton, Allen H. *Handicrafts of the Southern Highlands*. New York: Russell Sage Foundation, 1937.

Edwards, A. S. and L. Jones. "An Experimental and Field Study of North Georgia Mountaineers," *Journal of Social Psychology*, 9:317-333. 1938.

Erasmus, C. J. "Work Patterns in a Mayo Village," *American Anthropologist*, 57:322-333. 1955.

Evans-Pritchard, E. E. *The Nuer*. Oxford: Clarendon Press, 1940.

Fenneman, Nevin M. *Physiography of Eastern United States*. New York: McGraw-Hill Book Company, 1938.

Frost, N.   *A Statistical Study of the Public Schools of the Southern Appalachian Mountains*. U. S. Bureau of Education, Bulletin for 1915, No. 11. Washington: Government Printing Office, 1915.

Frothingham, E. H. *Timber Growing and Logging Practice in the Southern Appalachian Region.* U. S. Department of Agriculture, Technical Bulletin 250. Washington: Government Printing Office, 1931.

Gaumnitz, W. H. *Education in the Southern Mountains.* U. S. Department of Interior, Office of Education, Bulletin for 1937, No. 26. Washington: Government Printing Office, 1938.

Giffin, Roscoe. "Down in the Valley," *Mountain Life & Work,* 29, No. 1:39-46, No. 3:33-40, No. 4:38-46. 1953.

Gilliam, Lena. "A Contraceptive Service for Mountain Women," *Journal of Contraception,* 3:56-59. 1938.

Glendinning, R. M. "Spann: A Community Study in the Cumberland Plateau of Kentucky," *Papers of the Michigan Academy of Science, Arts and Letters,* 14:329-341. 1930.

———— and E. N. Torbert. "Agricultural Problems in Grainger County, Tennessee," *Economic Geography,* 14:159-166. 1938.

Glenn, L. C. *Denudation and Erosion of the Southern Appalachian Region and the Monongahela River.* U. S. Geological Survey Professional Papers, No. 72. Washington: Government Printing Office, 1911.

————. "The Physiographic Influences in the Development of Tennessee," *The Resources of Tennessee,* 5, No. 2:44-63. 1915.

Goodrich, Carter, et al. *Migration and Economic Opportunity.* Philadelphia: University of Pennsylvania Press, 1936.

Goodrich, Frances L. *Mountain Homespun.* New Haven: Yale University Press, 1931.

Gray, Lewis C. *History of Agriculture in the Southern United States to 1860.* Carnegie Institution of Washington Publications, No. 430. Washington, 1933.

Gray, W. T. "Population Movements in the Kentucky Mountains," *Rural Sociology,* 10:380-386. 1945.

————. "Factors Affecting Teacher Tenure in the Appalachian Highlands," *Rural Sociology,* 13:295-307. 1948.

Hall, Joseph S. *The Phonetics of Great Smoky Mountain Speech.* New York: King's Crown Press, 1942.

Hall, R. C. *Preliminary Study of Forest Conditions in Tennessee.* Tennessee Geological Survey, Bulletin 10. Nashville, 1910.

Haney, William H. *Mountain People of Kentucky.* Cincinnati: Roessler Bros., 1906.

Hatcher, O. L., ed. *A Mountain School.* Richmond: Garrett & Massie, Inc., 1930.

Haun, Mildred. *The Hawk's Done Gone.* Indianapolis: Bobbs-Merrill Company, Inc., 1940.

Hayes, C. W. *The Southern Appalachians.* National Geographic Society Monographs, No. 10, 1895.

Haywood, John. *The Civil and Political History of the State of Tennessee.* Knoxville: Heiskell & Brown, 1823.

Heberle, Rudolf. *The Impact of the War on Population Redistribution in the South.* Institute of Research and Training in the Social Sciences Papers, No. 7. Nashville: Vanderbilt University Press, 1945.

Heflin, C. and H. W. Beers. *Urban Adjustments of Rural Migrants; A Study of 297 Families in Lexington, Kentucky, 1942.* Kentucky Agricultural Experiment Station, Bulletin 487. Lexington, 1946.

Herring, Harriet L. *Passing of the Mill Villages.* Chapel Hill: University of North Carolina Press, 1949.

Herskovits, M. J. *Economic Anthropology.* New York: Alfred A. Knopf, Inc., 1952.

Hills, J. L., C. E. Wait and H. C. White. *Dietary Studies in Rural Regions in Vermont, Tennessee, and Georgia.* U. S. Department of Agriculture, Office of Experiment Stations, Bulletin 221. Washington: Government Printing Office, 1909.

Hirsch, N. D. M. "Experimental Study of the East Kentucky Mountains; A Study in Heredity and Environment," *Genetic Psychology Monographs,* 3:189-244. 1928.

Hitch, Margaret. "Life in a Blue Ridge Hollow," *Journal of Geography,* 30:309-322. 1931.

Hooker, Elizabeth R. *Religion in the Highlands.* New York: Home Mission Council, 1933.

Horn, Stanley F. *This Fascinating Lumber Business*. New York: Bobbs-Merrill Company, Inc. 1943.

Hundley, John R. "The Mountain Man in Northern Industry," *Mountain Life & Work*, 31, No. 2:33-38. 1955.

Jackson, George P. *White Spirituals in the Southern Uplands*. Chapel Hill: University of North Carolina Press, 1933.

Johnson, C. S., et al. *Statistical Atlas of Southern Counties*. Chapel Hill: University of North Carolina Press, 1941.

Kephart, Horace. *Our Southern Highlanders*. New York: Outing, 1913.

Killian, Lewis N. "Southern White Laborers in Chicago's West Side." Unpublished Ph.D. dissertation, University of Chicago, 1949.

————. "The Adjustment of Southern White Migrants to Northern Urban Norms," *Social Forces*, 32:66-69. 1953.

✓King, A. R. "A Note on Emergent Folk Cultures and World Culture Change," *Social Forces*, 31:234-237. 1953.

Knox, John B. *The People of Tennessee*. Knoxville: University of Tennessee Press, 1949.

Lanman, Charles. *Letters from the Alleghany Mountains*. New York: George Putnam, 1849.

Larson, O. F. "Wartime Migration and the Manpower Reserve on Farms in Eastern Kentucky," *Rural Sociology*, 8:148-161. 1943.

Lemert, B. F. *The Cotton Textile Industry of the Southern Appalachian Piedmont*. Chapel Hill: University of North Carolina Press, 1933.

Lewis, Claudia. *Children of the Cumberland*. New York: Columbia University Press, 1946.

Leybourne, G. G. "Urban Adjustments of Migrants from the Southern Appalachian Plateaus," *Social Forces*, 16:238-246. 1937.

Leyburn, James G. *Frontier Folkways*. New Haven: Yale University Press, 1935.

Loomis, C. P. and L. S. Dodson. *Standards of Living in Four Southern Appalachian Mountain Counties*. U. S. Department of Agriculture, Farm Security Administration, and Bureau of Agricultural Economics, Social Research Report 10. Washington: Government Printing Office, 1938.

Leubke, B. H. "Problems Created by the Douglas Reservoir in East Tennessee," *Journal of the Tennessee Academy of Sciences*, 29: 246-259. 1954.

————, et al. *Types of Farming in Tennessee.* Tennessee Agricultural Experiment Station, Bulletin 169. Knoxville, 1939.

MacClintock, S. S. "Kentucky Mountains and Their Feuds," *American Journal of Sociology*, 7:1-28, 171-187. 1901.

MacDonald, Lois. *Southern Mill Hills.* New York: Alex L. Hillman, 1928.

Mason, Robert L. *The Lure of the Great Smokies.* Boston: Houghton Mifflin Company, 1927.

Masters, F. N. and C. E. Allred. *The Cumberland Plateau in Tennessee.* Tennessee Agricultural Experiment Station, Bulletin 192. Knoxville, 1944.

Matthews, M. T. *Experience Worlds of Mountain People.* New York: Columbia University Press, 1937.

Miller, Nora. *The Girl in the Rural Family.* Chapel Hill: University of North Carolina Press, 1935.

Miner, Horace. "The Folk-Urban Continuum," *American Sociological Review*, 17:529-537. 1952.

Montgomery, James E. "Two Resettlement Communities on the Cumberland Plateau." Unpublished Master's thesis, Vanderbilt University, 1941.

————. "Three Appalachian Communities; Cultural Differentials as They Affect Levels of Living and Population Pressure." Unpublished Ph.D. dissertation, Vanderbilt University, 1944.

————. "Three Southern Appalachian Communities; An Analysis of Cultural Variables," *Rural Sociology*, 14:138-148. 1949.

———— and O. Leonard. "Settlement and Post-War Planning," *Applied Anthropology*, 3, No. 2:23-26. 1944.

Mooers, C. A. *Soils of Tennessee.* Tennessee Agricultural Experiment Station, Circular of Information 5. Knoxville, 1932.

Morgan, A. E. "Sociology in the TVA," *American Sociological Review*, 2:157-165. 1937.

Morley, Margaret W. *The Carolina Mountains*. Boston: Houghton Mifflin Company, 1913.

Murphy, R. E. "A Southern West Virginia Mining Community," *Economic Geography*, 9:51-59. 1933.

Nicholls, W. D. and J. H. Bondurant. *Farm Management and Family Incomes in Eastern Kentucky*. Kentucky Agricultural Experiment Station, Bulletin 491. Lexington, 1946.

———— and H. W. Hawthorne. *Farm Management and Incomes of Farm Families in Laurel County, Kentucky*. Kentucky Agricultural Experiment Station, Bulletin 305. Lexington, 1930.

———— and W. L. Rouse. *Farm Organizations and Family Incomes in Knott County, Ky.* Kentucky Agricultural Experiment Station, Bulletin 351. Lexington, 1934.

———— et al. *Family Incomes and Land Utilization in Knott County, Ky.* Kentucky Agricultural Experiment Station, Bulletin 375. Lexington, 1937.

Nienburg, Bertha M. *Potential Earning Power of Southern Mountaineer Handicrafts*. U. S. Department of Labor, Women's Bureau, Bulletin 128. Washington: Government Printing Office, 1935.

Odum, Howard D. "Notes on the Study of Regional and Folk Society," *Social Forces*, 10:164-175. 1931.

————. *Southern Regions of the United States*. Chapel Hill: University of North Carolina Press, 1936.

Olmsted, Frederick L. *Journey in the Back Country*. New York: Mason Brothers, 1860.

Owsley, Frank L. "Patterns of Migration and Settlement on the Southern Frontiers," *Journal of Southern History*, 11:147-176. 1945.

————. *Plain Folk of the Old South*. Baton Rouge: Louisiana State University Press, 1949.

Oyler, Merton. *Cost of Living and Population Trends in Laurel*

County, Kentucky. Kentucky Agricultural Experiment Station, Bulletin 301. Lexington, 1929.

————. *The Standard of Living of Farm Families in Grayson County, Kentucky.* Kentucky Agricultural Experiment Station, Bulletin 316. Lexington, 1931.

————. *Community and Neighborhood Grouping in Knott County, Kentucky.* Kentucky Agricultural Experiment Station, Bulletin 366. Lexington, 1936.

Parsons, Talcott. "The Kinship System of the Contemporary United States," *American Anthropologist,* 45:22-38. 1943.

Patton, James W. *Unionism and Reconstruction in Tennessee 1860-1869.* Chapel Hill: University of North Carolina Press, 1934.

Peattie, Roderick, ed. *The Great Smokies and the Blue Ridge.* New York: The Vanguard Press, 1943.

Peck, M., B. Frank and P. A. Eke. *Economic Utilization of Marginal Lands in Nicholas and Webster Counties, W. Va.* U. S. Department of Agriculture, Technical Bulletin 303. Washington: Government Printing Office, 1932.

Poole, Ernest. *Nurses on Horseback.* New York: The Macmillan Company, 1932.

Pope, Liston. *Millhands and Preachers.* New Haven: Yale University Press, 1942.

Potwin, Marjorie A. *Cotton Mill People of the Piedmont.* New York: Columbia University Press, 1927.

Quarles, Mary A. "A Comparison of Some Aspects of Family Life Between Two Areas of Leslie County, Kentucky." Unpublished Master's thesis, University of Kentucky, 1952.

————. "When Roads Come," *Mountain Life & Work,* 31, No. 2:40-43. 1955.

Raine, James W. *The Land of Saddle-bags.* New York: Council of Women for Home Missions, 1924.

Rambo, Marion Y. "The Submerged Tenth Among the Southern Mountaineers," *Methodist Review,* 87:565-575. 1905.

Ramsey, J. G. M. *The Annals of Tennessee.* Charleston, S. C.: Walker & James, 1853.

Randolph, Vance. *Ozark Mountain Folks*. New York: The Vanguard Press, 1932.

——. *Ozark Superstitions*. New York: Columbia University Press, 1947.

Redfield, Robert. *The Folk Culture of Yucatan*. Chicago: University of Chicago Press, 1941.

——. "The Folk Society," *American Journal of Sociology*, 52: 293-308. 1947.

——. "The Natural History of the Folk Society," *Social Forces*, 31:224-228. 1953.

——. *The Primitive World and Its Transformations*. Ithaca: Cornell University Press, 1953.

——. *The Little Community*. Chicago: University of Chicago Press, 1955.

Rhyne, Jennings J. *Some Southern Cotton Mill Workers and Their Villages*. Chapel Hill: University of North Carolina Press, 1930.

Roberts, Lydia. *The Nutrition and Care of Children in a Mountain County of Kentucky*. U. S. Department of Labor, Children's Bureau, Publication 110. Washington: Government Printing Office, 1922.

Ross, Malcolm. *Machine Age in the Hills*. New York: The Macmillan Company, 1933.

Satterfield, M. H. "The Removal of Families from Tennessee Valley Authority Reservoir Areas," *Social Forces*, 16:258-261. 1937.

Schockel, B. H. "Changing Conditions in the Kentucky Mountains," *Scientific Monthly*, 3:105-131. 1916.

Semple, Ellen C. "The Anglo-Saxons of the Kentucky Mountains; a Study in Anthropogeography," *Geographic Journal*, 17:588-623. 1901.

——. *American History and Its Geographic Conditions*. Boston: Houghton Mifflin Company, 1903.

Sharp, Cecil J. *Folk Songs from the Southern Appalachians*, edited by Maud Karpeles. New York: Oxford University Press, 1952.

Sheppard, Muriel E. *Cabins in the Laurel*. Chapel Hill: University of North Carolina Press, 1935.

Sherman, Mandel and T. R. Henry. *Hollow Folk.* New York: Thomas Y. Crowell Company, 1933.

———— and C. B. Key. "The Intelligence of Isolated Mountain Children," *Child Development,* 3:279-290. 1932.

Spalding, Arthur W. *The Hills o' Ca'liny.* Washington: Review & Herald, 1921.

Steele, Glenn. *Maternity and Infant Care in a Mountain County in Georgia.* U. S. Department of Labor, Children's Bureau, Publication 120. Washington : Government Printing Office, 1923.

Sweet, William W. *Religion in Colonial America.* New York: Charles Scribner's Sons, 1942.

————. *Religion in the Development of American Culture, 1765-1840.* New York: Charles Scribner's Sons, 1952.

Taeuber, Conrad. "Agricultural Underemployment," *Rural Sociology,* 8:342-355. 1943.

Tax, Sol. "World View and Social Relations in Guatemala," *American Anthropologist,* 43:27-42. 1941.

————, ed. *Heritage of Conquest.* Glencoe, Ill.: The Free Press, 1952.

Taylor, C. C., et al. *Disadvantaged Classes in American Agriculture.* U. S. Department of Agriculture, Farm Security Administration, and Bureau of Agricultural Economics, Social Research Report 8. Washington: Government Printing Office, 1938.

————. *Rural Life in the United States.* New York: Alfred A. Knopf, Inc., 1949.

Taylor, George R., ed. *The Turner Thesis.* Boston: D. C. Heath and Company, 1949.

Thompson, Samuel H. *The Highlanders of the South.* New York: Eaton & Mains, 1910.

Tiffany, E. L. "Selling Health in the Mountains," *Public Health Nursing,* 31:89-92. 1939.

Turner, Frederick J. *The Frontier in American History.* New York: Henry Holt and Company, 1920.

————. *The Significance of Sections in American History.* New York: Peter Smith, 1950.

U. S. Department of Agriculture, Bureau of Agricultural Economics, *Economic and Social Problems and Conditions of the Southern Appalachians*. U. S. Department of Agriculture, Miscellaneous Publications 205. Washington: Government Printing Office, 1935.

Vance, Rupert B. *Regional Reconstruction: A Way Out for the South*. Chapel Hill: University of North Carolina Press, 1935.

————. *Human Geography of the South*. Chapel Hill: University of North Carolina Press, 1935.

————. *All These People*. Chapel Hill: University of North Carolina Press, 1945.

Verhoeff, Mary. *Kentucky Mountains; Transportation and Commerce, 1750-1911*. Filson Club Publications, No. 26. Louisville: John P. Morton, 1911.

————. *The Kentucky River Navigation*. Filson Club Publications, No. 28. Louisville: John P. Morton, 1917.

Vincent, G. E. "A Retarded Frontier: Kentucky," *American Journal of Sociology*, 4:1-20. 1898.

Voget, Fred W. "The Folk Society—an Anthropological Application," *Social Forces*, 33:105-113. 1954.

Warner, Charles D. *On Horseback*. Boston: Houghton Mifflin Company, 1889.

Wheeler, Lester R. "The Intelligence of East Tennessee Mountain Children," *Journal of Educational Psychology*, 23:351-370. 1932.

————. "A Study of the Remote Mountain People of the Tennessee Valley," *Journal of the Tennessee Academy of Sciences*, 10:33-36. 1935.

————. "Changes in the Dietary Habits of Remote Mountain People Since 1900," *Journal of the Tennessee Academy of Sciences*, 10:167-174. 1935.

White, Edwin E. *Highland Heritage*. New York: Friendship Press, 1937.

————. "Religious Ideals in the Highlands," *Mountain Life & Work*, 27, No. 4:26-31. 1951.

Willeford, Mary B. *Income and Health in Remote Rural Areas.* New York: Frontier Nursing Service, 1932.

Williams, Faith, et al. *Family Living in Knott County, Kentucky.* U. S. Department of Agriculture, Technical Bulletin 576. Washington: Government Printing Office, 1937.

Williams, Samuel. *History of the Lost State of Franklin.* Johnson City, Tenn.: Watauga Press, 1924.

————. *Dawn of Tennessee Valley and Tennessee History.* Johnson City, Tenn.: Watauga Press, 1937.

————. *Tennessee During the Revolutionary War.* Nashville: Tennessee Historical Commission, 1944.

————, ed. *Early Travels in the Tennessee Country.* Johnson City, Tenn.: Watauga Press, 1928.

Wilson, Samuel T. *The Southern Mountaineers.* New York: Presbyterian Home Missions, 1906.

Wood, Hariette. "The Kentucky Mountains." Unpublished Master's thesis, University of North Carolina, 1930.

Woofter, T. J., Jr. "Tennessee Valley Regional Plan," *Social Forces,* 12:329-338. 1933.

————. "Rural Relief and the Back-to-the-Farm-Movement," *Social Forces,* 14:382-388. 1936.

Zimmerman, C. C. and M. E. Frampton. *Family and Society.* New York: D. Van Nostrand Company, Inc., 1935.